MAX SCHELER'S CONCEPT OF THE PERSON

Max Scheler's Concept of the Person

An Ethics of Humanism

Ron Perrin
Professor of Political Theory
University of Montana
Missoula, U.S.A.

St. Martin's Press   New York

First published in the United States of America in 1991

Printed in Hong Kong

ISBN 0–312–05308–8

Library of Congress Cataloguing-in-Publication Data
Perrin, Ron, 1934–   .
Max Scheler's concept of the person : an ethics of humanism / Ron
Perrin.
   p.   cm.
Includes bibliographical references and index.
ISBN 0–312–05308–8
1. Scheler, Max, 1874–1928—Ethics.   2. Ethics, Modern—19th
century.   3. Ethics, Modern—20th century.   4. Philosophical
anthropology.   I. Title.
B3329.S484P47   1991
170'.92—dc20   90–43341
                                                            CIP

For Sandra and Sasha

Contents

Preface

... man is more of a problem to himself at the present time than ever before in all recorded history. At the very moment when man admits that he knows less than ever about himself, and when he is not frightened by any possible answer to the question, there seems to have arisen a new courage of truthfulness – a courage to raise the essential question without any commitment to any tradition, whether theological, philosophical or scientific, that has prevailed up to now. At the same time he is developing a new kind of self-consciousness and insight into his own nature based on the vast accumulation of knowledge in the new human sciences.

Max Scheler
Man's Place in Nature

Max Scheler was born in 1874 and he died in 1928. His life was shorter than many but far richer than most. Into his 56 years he managed to pack three marriages and two religious conversions, a host of love affairs, and a teaching career which embraced four universities, lecture halls throughout Europe and innumerable cafés. And then there is his writing: 13 volumes worth, which reveal a restless and often violently contradictory nature. War and pacifism, asceticism and sensuality, catholicism and pantheism; each of these themes received the concentrated attention of his mind and, in turn, made lasting demands upon his soul. But if his life's work displays a spirit often at odds with itself, it also bespeaks an effort to faithfully record all that comes within the compass of human experience. It is here, in his persistent concern for what he calls 'the problem of man' that we find the unifying thread of Scheler's life and thought.

Like his contemporary, Edmund Husserl, Scheler saw the state of philosophy and science at the dawn of the twentieth century as one of critical disarray. But his attention to the human condition led him to interpret the conflicts and uncertainties that afflicted these disciplines as both counterpoint and contributor to a far more primordial crisis, a *désordre du coeur*, which distorted and perverted Man's vision prior to the formulation of any given theory of knowledge or of any science.[1]

In Scheler's view, this distortion was most evident in the Kantian portrayal of Man as, in essence, an autonomous rationality; an image that effectively left the human being stranded on the shoals of Reason's self-governing and self-limiting principles and functions. In order to once again speak to the total Man – the loving, willing, creating, *living* human being – Scheler challenged himself and philosophy to think anew. We must, he insisted, approach the problems of philosophy and the world with a new and transformed consciousness, one that would listen and heed the voices of Man's entire environment. For example, Scheler was convinced that once philosophy was free of its Kantian presuppositions it would gain accesss to a hitherto unknown and *a priori* realm of values, values that are immediately given in our most primal and immediate experience of things and others.

In his effort to support these claims and demands Scheler did not hesitate to draw freely upon the insights and achievements of disciplines beyond philosophy. His work is richly larded with evidence from theology and psychology, as well as from the social and natural sciences. And, as his curiosity refused to accept the constraints of the academic division of labour, so too it would not easily accept the confining boundaries of any single philosophical school. At various points, and with what were often remarkably differing results, transcendental idealism and British empiricism, phenomenology and *Lebensphilosophie*, were among the many contributors to Scheler's unique *Weltanschauung*. But, Scheler was no undisciplined eclecticist. Rather, his approach is akin to that of the artist who selects from his or her pallet those shadings of colour which can best lend substance to the vision. Scheler's vision was large and fresh: its expression demanded a pallet of many and various hues.

One possible misconception must be laid to rest at the outset of our study. Scheler's treatment of his philosophical forebears was neither frivolous nor disrespectful. On the contrary, few thinkers have ever demonstrated a greater esteem for the past. Scheler well knew that any contribution he might make towards humankind's expanding self-awareness, no matter how radically it might seem to depart from the tradition, would not be in the manner of a creation *ex nihilo*. Instead, it would involve a rediscovery of capacities and modes of expression long inherent in the human condition, and the regaining of a philosophical stance that might point the way towards their fulfilment.

This, then, is some of the mood and purpose that characterises Scheler's thought. In the work at hand we shall find that some of the themes to which he devoted himself are thoroughly developed, while others demand a further elaboration that will thrust us beyond Scheler and into our own time and space. While this move may at first seem to take us far beyond the scene in which he moved, in a deeper sense there is no change in context between his world and ours. For who can deny that our politics and ethics, in disjointed concert with our technology and our ecology, are in disarray, and that the crucial task of philosophy is still the articulation of the human condition: of what it is and what it might become?

The dominant theme of this study, and the vehicle by which I propose to draw Scheler into the crises of our time, is his concept of the Person. Increasingly, those who are most wary of the events and forces that have come to define the present age are prompted to echo an admonition uttered by Lewis Mumford some thirty years ago. In *The City in History* Mumford called attention to:

> an ultimate decision that confronts man and (that) will, one way or another, ultimately transform him: namely, whether he shall devote himself to the development of his own deepest humanity, or whether he shall surrender himself to the now almost automatic forces he himself has set in motion and yield place to his dehumanized alter ego, 'Post-historic man'. That second choice will bring with it a progressive loss of feeling, emotion, creative audacity, and finally, consciousness.[2]

Fortunately we have projects such as Scheler's to help us in charting the alternative to this second choice. As his concept of the Person unfolds we will find him striving over and over again to sound the depths of that deepest humanity of which Mumford speaks. To be sure, Scheler's reflections often lead him down false paths and, occasionally, to the brink of failure. Yet, as with all pioneers, the way of those who follow is made surer and safer if they will but take the time to observe and learn.

Acknowledgements

It was Herbert Marcuse who first encouraged me to undertake the study of Scheler's ethical writings. For that, and for many other kindnesses, both professional and personal, he occupies a very special place in my memories. Along the way I was also encouraged in this effort by Harry Hausser and Calvin Schrag. The friendship and help of Ulrich Klee have been invaluable resources, as has the more tangible support provided during the summer of 1989 by my Dean, James Flightner.

Lastly, the assistance of Kermit Hummel at St. Martin's Press, the kind words of Pauline Snelson, and the patient care of my editor, Sophie Lillington, have made it possible for me to bring this work to its present stage. None of them, of course, bear any responsibility for whatever shortcomings the reader may find.

Permissions

An earlier version of chapter 2 appeared in *Philosophy Research Archives*, Vol. 1 (1975) and an earlier version of chapter 3 in *The Journal of the History of Philosophy*, Vol. XII, No. 3 (July 1974). Permission has been granted to incorporate those materials into the present study.

Introduction

Max Scheler's major work, and the only one he felt he had satisfactorily carried through to completion, is *Der Formalismus in der Ethik und die materiale Wertethik*.[1] Here, in various stages of development, we find all of the themes which occupied Scheler's philosophical attention, as well as his most sustained reflections on the nature of the Person. As the title suggests, the book is a pivotal work. Scheler engages in a lengthy and detailed assessment of the main premises, strengths, and failings of ethical formalism before undertaking his own attempt to formulate an ethic grounded in the intuitive perception of values as real and substantial (*materiale*) qualities of normative experience.

At the outset, we must acknowledge that it is difficult to render the precise meaning of the German adjective *materiale* into English.[2] The English, 'objective', is misleading insofar as it implies a body in space and time which is subject to empirical confirmation, that is, whose existence can be certified by sight or touch. As we shall see, Scheler has something far more subtle in mind. On the other hand, a simple transliteration into the English 'material' is not altogether appropriate since the significance of the term, when applied to values, is far from clear. I have, however, chosen to adopt the latter approach and to proceed on the assumption that the lack of any immediate meaning is less likely to confuse than the presence of the wrong one. If we begin with as few preconceptions as possible, perhaps we will more readily come to understand the term as Scheler intended. This strategy is further justified – if not necessitated –by the fact that Scheler offers us no clear and final definition. Instead, his conceptualisation of a *materiale Wertethik* evolves out of his reflections – specifically, from his critical reflections on ethical formalism – and, therefore, an adequate understanding of this concept can come only with and through a consideration of that critique.

Nonetheless, to begin with as few preconceptions as possible is not to begin in a vacuum. The contrast is Scheler's title between formal and material ethics offers a clue to his intention, insofar as it recalls the distinction Kant drew between the form and the content of experience. For when Scheler writes of ethical

1

formalism it is Kant's ethics which he has in mind; we are, then, safe in *provisionally* assuming that, following Kant's lead, one concern of the *materiale Wertethik* will be with that which is given in sensibility rather than that which is contributed to experience by the understanding. Thus, one motive for beginning this study with a review of Kant reflects the terminological kinship between him and Scheler: a clarification of Kant's arguments cannot help but contribute to a better comprehension of Scheler's.

There are other reasons for devoting considerable attention to Kant. For one, Scheler's critique of Kant is liberally studded with what appear to be off-hand references to the latter's position. More often than not these allusions are undocumented, leaving the reader with the task of determining whether Kant ever made the claims Scheler attributes to him and, if so, in what context. Hopefully, a review of Kant that highlights those themes which concern Scheler will make it easier to determine when, and if, he is misappropriating Kant, without forcing us into long digressions of textual exegesis. Furthermore, in many cases Scheler clearly is not referring to the letter of the Kantian ethic but, rather, to what he considers its presuppositions. Unless the reader brings to the study of Scheler a reasonably clear image of Kant's philosophical system it is often difficult to identify exactly what Scheler is referring to.

Third, in the all too limited body of English language commentary on Scheler, there is no attempt to assess the merits or demerits of Scheler's Kant-critique.[3] Yet, as one such commentator notes, many of Scheler's arguments in this regard are questionable. While an exhaustive treatment of the subject is beyond the scope of the present study, it seems worthwhile to begin the task of unravelling what might eventually become a contentious theme in Kant scholarship.

My final reason for beginning with a consideration of Scheler's Kant-critique reflects my conviction that any philosophical position which incorporates an elaborate analysis of some contrary position will, no matter how extreme the points of contention, be circumscribed in some measure by the very arguments with which it contends. These constitute a large part of any philosophy's environment: we can no more understand the philosophy in isolation from them than we can appreciate the cactus without knowing something of the desert within which it grows and against which it struggles. It will be one of my tasks within this study to show how this is particularly true of Scheler's relationship with Kant.

By underscoring the Kantian influence on Scheler's material ethic and its theory of the Person I am, of course, thereby circumscribing my own study. Within the context of the present work it does not seem salient to consider alternative philosophies of the person and personality. Among the former, the most ambitious instance is Derek Parfit's *Reasons and Persons*.[4] Parfit's effort is a remarkable *tour de force* of analytic philosophy, which exposes the logical inconsistencies that necessarily accompany any attempt to ground personal identity in the existence of some separate entity – for example, the 'soul' or the 'self' – that persists within or behind the individual's experience of his or her physical and psychological continuity. Indeed, in Parfit's 'reductionist' understanding of the Person, the only convincing evidence that can be mounted in defence of personal identity comes from a careful consideration of just what the nature of physical and psychological continuity consists of.

This attempt to uncouple our beliefs about the Person from their subtle and tenuous link with the presumption of a Cartesian-like ego is not altogether removed from Scheler's own effort to re-think the foundations and claims of personalist philosophy. However, in contrast to the considerations and possibilities that come before us when we begin reflecting upon Scheler's person-alism, I find Parfit's philosophy unduly sparse. The strength of his analysis, as is typical of the best works in the analytic tradition, is therapeutic, in so far as it cleanses conventional wisdom of many of its most insupportable beliefs and assumptions. We are left, however, with the answer to a philosophical puzzle rather than an understanding of the Person that might serve the task of reconstructing a moral philosophy that would address the normative dimension of life in all of its rich, and yes, maddening extravagance.

Similar considerations have prompted me to forego consid-eration of that variety of personalism that is addressed to the relationship between personality and politics.[5] As we shall see, Scheler does invite us to reflect upon this relationship. But, in contrast to the prevailing literature on personality and politics, he is not concerned to analyse the consequences of individual personality for political action or the effect of personality types, for example, the authoritarian personality, upon political policies and cultures. Rather, he offers us a provocative and problematic way of understanding communities and states as the expressions of 'collective Persons'.

A final observation on the title of this work may be in order. With Michel Foucault, I recognise that the term 'humanism' is extraordinarily 'supple' and 'diverse'.[6] Nonetheless, to the extent that it calls the readers attention to Scheler's *attempt* to ground his ethics squarely within the context of the human condition, and thereby to eschew any conditional references or appeals to a reality beyond that present in our lived humanity, I find the characterisation of his ethics as a 'humanism' appropriate. As we shall see, he is not wholly successful in his endeavour. I believe, however, that he has pointed the study of ethics in the direction it ought to pursue.

Part I
Scheler's Critique of Kant

1

The Ethical Implications of Kant's First Critique

THE CASE AGAINST EMPIRICISM

To read Kant's mature (post-critical) ethics if to journey through a philosophical purgatory. His intention is to construct a pure moral philosophy and, to this end, he seeks nothing less than to cleanse ethics from 'that lax and even mean habit of thought which seeks for its principles amongst empirical motives and laws', which 'substitutes for morality a bastard patched up from limbs of various derivations, which looks like anything one chooses to see in it, only not like virtue to one who had once beheld her in her true form'.[1] These are strong sentiments for the supposedly cool and dispassionate sage of Konigsberg. In order to understand the disdain with which he views the prospect of those ethics that are grounded in our experience of the phenomenal world, it is necessary to know something of the role he assigns to empirical motives and laws in his own system of philosophy.

In both his *Fundamental Principles of the Metaphysics of Morals* and the *Critique of Practical Reason*, Kant repeatedly expresses his objection to any moral principles that are derived from empirical motives. Among his various arguments in this regard, one of the most succinct occurs within the context of the first and second theorems of the *critique*. Here Kant contends that any actions primarily concerned with the realisation of some object or state of sensibility are impelled by the anticipated pleasure which the action will bring to its subject. However, we can never know in advance of the action itself whether it will bring pleasure, pain or, indeed, whether we will be affected one way or the other. I might, for example, anticipate that a Mexican vacation or the fulfilling of my promise to present a guest lecture in a colleague's course will be pleasurable or gratifying. Yet, only after I have undertaken the trip or presented the lecture will I learn whether my anticipations were correct. In either case, my knowledge is contingent upon experience and contributes little to my understanding of the world. If the vacation were satisfying but the lecture less than gratifying, the next time it might be wholly different. Thus, Kant would conclude, any principles which might be derived from such experiences will be *a posteriori* and cannot possibly serve as sure and invariable guides *to* action, that is, as practical laws.

What is more, pleasure and pain are wholly subjective and private states of sensibility that vary in degree (and often in kind) from one individual to the next. One man's pleasure is another's poison. Any principle grounded in what contributes to the pleasure of an individual is relative to a host of possible interests and proclivities and, once again, can never provide objective and universal norms which might govern the behaviour of all human beings. Hence, Kant's objection to empirical motives – and with this his rejection of any utilitarian ethics – reflects his contention that whatever understanding these might provide will be either contingent or relative; the very antithesis of the universal and necessary (*a priori*) knowledge for which a genuine morality must strive.

In my judgement these arguments, as Kant presents them in the second *Critique*, are not especially persuasive. The utilitarian might well object, for example, that an inductive analysis of experience can provide a safe guide to moral practices; as when inveterate liars eventually discover that they are unable to fashion any lasting and secure social relationships. Only if we accept the Theorem from which Kant's observations are derived; namely, that 'all practical principles which presuppose an object (*materie*) of the faculty of desire as the ground of determination of the will are empirical, and can furnish no practical laws',[2] are we likely to concur with his conclusions. But, within the context of the second *Critique* there seems to be no compelling reason to accept the Theorem. However, as soon as we recall that the points he is making are consistent and logical applications of the analysis of experience he developed earlier in the *Critique of Pure Reason*, his case is considerably enhanced.

A fundamental tenet of the *Critique of Pure Reason* holds that the immediately given material of sensation is a necessary but insufficient element for all scientific knowledge.[3] True, the data presented in sense experience are intuited within the manifold of space and time: without the intuition of space we would be unable to represent objects as outside us; without the intuition of time, our sense experience would be bereft of either sequence or concurrence. Space and time, then, are minimal conditions of experience. But without the conceptual activity of the Understanding (*Verstand*) sensibility would remain blind. Strictly speaking, we would not even have a coherent experience if we were limited to what is present in sensibility. 'Experience', Kant writes, 'contains two very dissimilar elements, namely, the *matter* of knowledge (obtained) from the senses, and a certain *form* for the ordering of this matter (obtained) from the inner source of pure intuition and thought which, on the occasion of the sense-impressions, are first brought into action and yield concepts'. (A 86) Despite the refined distinctions he draws between the spatio-temporal manifold, as a formal condition for the possibility of objective experience, and the formal coherence which thought imposes upon this experience, Kant's point is deceptively simple. Experience, as we come to 'know' it, is a composite of objects and relationships between them which, if not given in sensible intuition, must be credited to the activity of an Understanding that imposes a formal structure upon the raw material of sensation. The existence of an object (that is, its extended presence in space), indeed the very possibility of experience itself, requires that the material of sensation conform to such concepts as 'extension', in other words, to conceptual conditions which are not given in mere sensibility but are rather the *a priori* contributions of thought. (A93, B 126)

The implications of this analysis upon the subject of our discussion is that the conditional character of any empirical motives that might presume to serve as the foundation for practical (ethical) laws becomes a consequence of the structure of experience itself. For, insofar as such motives are inextricably bound up with sensation they must share in the contingency of all things sensible and cannot, by definition, furnish *a priori* knowledge. This is, as I read Kant, the rationale behind his denial of any decisive ethical role to empirical motives, such as the expectation of happiness which the possession of some object or the performance of some action might bring.

Once this much is established, however, we must acknowledge that it accounts for only part of Kant's objections to any empirically established ethic. He is, as we have seen, equally concerned to deny any decisive role to empirical *laws*. Here again, I would suggest that his position can be clarified by consulting his analysis of experience.

We may begin by noting that the contingency which prevails between the formal and the material elements of experience is not unilateral. Matter stands in need of structure, yes; but it is also the case that without the material present in sensible intuition the formal elements of experience would have no substantial reality. While, in Kant's phrase, 'intuitions without concepts are blind, thoughts without content are empty. It is, therefore, just as necessary to make our concepts sensible, that is, to add the object to them in intuition, as to make our intuitions intelligible, that is, to bring them under concepts'. (A 51) This formulation is a bit misleading insofar as it implies that somehow conceptual understanding encounters an object which is already present in intuition. More precisely, as we have seen, all that is given in intuition is raw sensuous material; 'objective' only in the sense that it must be represented as outside us 'in space'. The situation is analogous to that of the weaver standing before a pile of flax. Just as the cloth which which he or she will eventually work must first be fashioned in the activity of spinning, so too the objects over which the Understanding will eventually pass judgement must be constituted in initial acts of conceptualisation. For example, 'it is the concept of "body" which necessitates the representation of extension, and therefore, representations of impenetrability, shape, etc.' (A 106). These are, again, minimal conditions to be met before we can even begin to speak meaningfully of objects, conditions which are provided by thought but not given with (nor are they to be equated with) the intuitive representation of space and time. However, more germaine to our problem is the function of concepts in determining relations between objects once the latter have been constituted. For it is here where the concepts serve as laws of experience. In order to explicate Kant's intention, and, in addition, introduce the empirical law with the greatest significance for his ethics, the following passage from the first *Critique* is helpful.

... the objective relation of appearances that follow upon one another is not to be determined through mere perception. In order that this relation be known as determined, the relation between the two states must be so thought that it is thereby determined as necessary which of them must be placed before, and which of them after, and that they cannot be placed in the reverse relation. But the concept which carries with it a necessity of synthetic unity can only be a pure concept that lies in the understanding, not in perception, and in this case it is the concept of the *relation of cause and effect*, the former of which determines the latter in time, as its consequence . . . Experience itself – in other words, empirical knowledge of appearances – is thus possible only insofar as we subject the succession of appearances, and therefore all alteration, to the law of causality; and, as likewise follows, *the appearances, as objects of experience* (my emphasis), are themselves possible only in conformity with the law. (B 234)

Here Kant is acknowledging and giving an account of the fact that sense experience not only requires the objective reality of a spatio-temporal realm 'occupied' as it were by objects and events; each, as we have seen, dependent upon the *a priori* contributions of intuition and the Understanding. Beyond this, in order for the perception of appearances to become a cognitive reality – and Kant makes clear in this passage his intention to equate experience with cognition – the warp and woof of sensory perception must be unified in schematic or relational fashion.

The driving example here is, of course, the relation of causality. But this relation is possible only by virtue of a more general feature of experience; namely, 'the *objective succession* of appearances'. (A 193). Our perceptions are determined, in *a priori* fashion by the sequential character of experience. In Kant's illustration, 'I see a ship move downstream. My perception of its lower position follows upon my perception of its position higher up in the stream, and it is impossible that in the apprehension of this appearance the ship should first be perceived lower down in the stream and afterwards higher up'. (A 192)

It is this lawlike character of sense-experience which, in effect, rescues consciousness from what would otherwise be either the sensation of chaos or the whimsy of an arbitrary subjectivity. ' . . . we must derive the *subjective succession* of apprehension from the *objective succession* of appearances. Otherwise the order of apprehension is entirely undetermined, and does not distinguish one appearance from another. Since the subjective succession by itself is altogether arbitrary, it does not prove anything . . . The objective succession will therefore consist in that order of the manifold of appearance according to which, *in conformity with a rule*, the apprehension of that which happens follows upon the apprehension of that which precedes'. (A 193)

Thus, for Kant, the experience of causality, and with it both the possibility and the knowledge of sense experience, *must* be attributed to the activity of the Understanding. 'We can extract clear concepts' (for example, causality) 'from experience, only because we have put them into experience, and because experience is thus brought about by their means.' (A 196) The consequences of this analysis are, of course, dramatic. Such a thoroughgoing conceptualisation of experience will ultimately entail the claim that 'nature, in the empirical sense, . . . the connection of appearances as regards their existence according to necessary rules', is contingent upon the Understanding. (A 216, B 263)

This decisive turn of thought away from any inductive philosophy of the natural sciences represents Kant's 'Copernican Revolution', in which 'objects must be viewed as conforming to human thought, not human thought to the independently real'.[4] While much has been written on the scientific implications of this development, noting, for example, how it is 'inspired by the avowed purpose of neutralizing the naturalistic implications of the Copernican astronomy',[5] we shall see that its implications are no less significant for ethics. But first we must consider why, if all objectivity, and ultimately nature itself, is constituted by the activity of thought upon sensibility, those laws which serve our theoretical knowledge cannot also suffice for practical knowledge?

The answer is an elaboration of our earlier observation that the contingency which prevails between the form and the matter of experience is reciprocal. In the Kantian schema, thought, in its theoretical or empirical mode, is limited by the conditions of experience. Thus, if the concept of causality is to have any substantial application or effectiveness, something must first be given to the Understanding through sensibility. 'If the reader will go back to the proof of the principle of causality . . . he will observe that we were able to prove it only of objects of possible experience, and even so, not from pure concepts, but only as a principle of the possibility of experience, and therefore of the knowledge of an object given in *empirical intuition*.'[6]

The end result of this state of affairs is a closed system; the

Understanding can never transcend the limits of experience and the material of such experience must conform to the principles of Understanding. Within the realm of the empirical, each constituent is governed by absolute and inviolable laws: there is no state, event, or object which is not strictly determined by its antecedent. To admit a single exception would cast nature and the comprehension of nature, that is, science, into perpetual confusion and doubt. But, where there is such absolute and universal determination, there is no possibility of rationally proclaiming that any condition or event is or ought to be preferred over any other. Those who would do so are addressing themselves to an imaginary world of their own making. The empirical world is simply there in all its unyielding facticity and, as a member of that world, what I am and what I do are nothing more than moments in a sequence of natural circumstances. And what are the consequences of such a condition for morality? Kant does not hesitate to draw the only possible conclusion: ' . . since the thorough-going connection of all appearances, in a context of nature, is an inexorable law, the inevitable consequence of obstinately insisting upon the reality of appearances is to destroy all freedom'. (A 537, B 565)

In light of this last claim my earlier characterisation of Kant's ethics as a purgatory should not seem too extreme. Once we accept his analysis of the empirical world, morality can only be affirmed, and freedom certified, through the denial of any exclusive or final reality to the realm of empirical nature and sensory experience.

Here we must pause to appreciate the irony of Kant's first *Critique*. With enormous toil and a series of philosophical reflections that are exquisite in their elaboration, he strives to rescue the claims of natural science from any possible scepticism. Yet, in doing so he severely limits the cognitive sway of empirical knowledge. Within the full range of the intellectual life, such knowledge makes important, and indeed, necessary, contributions. In the end, however, any pretence of scientific or empirical knowledge to instruct us in the way things really are – or sustain our interest in freedom – is soundly rejected. This is the deeper significance of Kant's Copernican Revolution: he is able to deny the finality of the world present in empirical knowledge and scientific understanding because he has never affirmed it in the first place.

What we have meant to say is that all our intuition is nothing

but the representation of appearance; that the things which we
intuit are not in themselves what we intuit them as being, nor
their relations so constituted in themselves as they appear to us,
and that if the subject, or even only the subjective constitution
of our senses in general, be removed, the whole constitution
and all the relations of objects in space and time, nay, space
and time themselves, would vanish. As appearances, they
cannot exist in themselves, but only in us. What objects
may be in themselves, and apart from all this receptivity
of our sensibility, remains completely unknown to us. We
know only our mode of perceiving them – a mode which
is peculiar to us, and not necessarily shared by every being,
though, certainly by every human being. (A 42)

THE TRANSCENDENTAL IDEA OF FREEDOM

The distinction Kant draws in this last passage, between the object
as it appears to us and the object as it is in itself, bespeaks the
fundamental dualism in his philosophy between the phenomenal
and the noumenal realms. So far we have considered only the
former, and found it characterised by a pervasive necessity: the
material of sensation must conform to the formal elements of
experience while, in their turn, these elements must confine their
application to that which is given in sensibility. However, just as
reality is not exhausted in experience, thought is not exhausted
in the activity, categories, and concepts of the Understanding.
Kant, it should be clear, is no solipsist. For every appearance
thought, in its *rational* capacity (namely as *Vernunft*) insists upon
positing the thing-in-itself as that which appears: for every series
of conditions Reason demands, 'by necessity and by right',
the unconditioned which is required to complete the series of
conditions. (B xx & B xxvi) Thus, Kant describes Reason, in the
Third Antinomy of Pure Reason, as confronting the unrelieved
causality which marks the phenomenal realm with the idea of a
spontaneous causality: the idea of a transcendental freedom.

It is important to avoid any impression that Kant's move from
the phenomenal to the noumenal realm is merely a device invoked
to provide some space for freedom in a system dominated by
necessity. Quite the contrary: as a transcendental idea or concept of Reason, 'freedom' is among those concepts which 'alone

make possible the totality of conditions . . . ' (B 379) Perhaps we can grasp more clearly that what is at stake here is the very *meaning* of the experiential world if we consider Kant's intention in light of Nietzsche's concept of the Eternal Recurrence. In *The Will to Power* Nietzsche writes, 'let us think this thought in its most terrible form: existence as it is, without meaning or aim, yet recurring inevitably without any finale of nothingness'.[7] Like Kant, Nietzsche recognises that thought cannot grasp or comprehend the prospect of an infinite becoming, that such an experience would be purposeless and devoid of any sense. But, where Nietzsche would have us abandon the comforting hypotheses of Reason – would plunge us into the stream of this endless process without purpose, to *suffer* existence – Kant remains with the demands of Reason and is driven to *think* of a peace beyond becoming in the purely intelligible realm of the absolute and transcendental. For Kant, unless we have recourse to the concept of a causality through freedom, and its corollary, the notion of a first cause, nature remains incomplete. We can give an explanation of particular events and appearances, but without the idea of some beginning and limit can never arrive at the prospect of nature as a totality, that is, of *a* world within which natural events and experiences occur. Hence, the transcendental idea of freedom is, for Kant, not some arbitrary fiction but, rather, a necessary postulate of Reason. (A 448, B 476–451, B 478)

Nonetheless, in a less dramatic fashion, Kant's conclusion is as disconcerting as Nietzsche's. For once we introduce into Kant's analysis of nature a single exception to the law of natural causality, chaos threatens, and we are, as it were, thrown back into that Humean universe in which there is no necessary ground for supposing that sunrise will follow sunset.

At this point it becomes crucial for Kant to maintain a rigid distinction between phenomenal and noumenal reality. The contradictions he encounters in attempting to sustain the opposing notions of a free and a natural causality on the same ontological plane are simply too immense. But, by maintaining a dualism between an intelligible realm which numbers among its relationships a causality through freedom and an experiential realm governed by natural causality the conflict is avoided.

> When we are dealing with what happens there are only two kinds of causality conceivable by us; the causality is either according to *nature* or arises from *freedom*. The former is the

connection in the sensible world of one state with a preceding state on which it follows according to a rule . . . By freedom, on the other hand . . . I understand the power of beginning a state *spontaneously* . . . Freedom, in this sense, is a pure transcendental idea, which, in the first place, contains nothing borrowed from experience, and which, secondly, refers to an object that cannot be determined or given in any experience. (A 532, B 560 – A 533, B 561)

The import of these claims becomes clear when we recall Kant's intention to construct a pure moral philosophy. For, with this definition of causality through freedom we have his first articulation of that pure concept – a concept which is neither grounded in, nor related to, the conditions, motives and laws of the empirical world – which will serve as the fulcrum upon which his formal ethics will turn. 'It should especially be noted that the practical concept of freedom is based upon this transcendental idea . . . ' But if the transcendental idea of freedom is the ground of practical freedom, it is also 'the real source of the difficulty by which the problem of freedom has always been beset'. (A 534, B 562) Again, Kant has been able to demonstrate the possibility of freedom only by sustaining a radical distinction between the phenomenal and noumenal realms. The difficulty to which he now refers is that once we assign freedom a place beyond the realm of experience, we encounter the problem of establishing the practical significance of such freedom for our intentions and actions within experience. Does, then, the discovery of freedom as a necessary and legitimate postulate of Reason bring us closer to the possibility of demonstrating that human beings, as members of the empirical world – and thereby subject to the laws of natural determination – are nonetheless morally free and responsible? These are the questions which Kant struggles to resolve in his subsequent ethical studies. But, before turning to those studies, we must note that there is at least an intimation of a solution in the first *Critique*.

MAN AS PHENOMENAL AND NOUMENAL BEING

In citing the conditions which would have to be met in order to bridge the gap between transcendental and natural causality, Kant observes that such conditions would involve finding some subject in the sensible world which has both an empirical and an intelligible character. The former would indicate that 'its actions, as appearances, stand in thoroughgoing connection with other appearances in accordance with unvarying laws of nature', the latter, 'that it is the cause of these same actions as appearances, but does not itself stand under any conditions of sensibility'. (A 539, B 567) In effect, then, such a subject would stand at the point of intersection between the phenomenal and noumenal realms. It seems superfluous to note that Kant does not have to seek far and wide for his subject . . .

Man is one of the appearances of the sensible world, and in so far one of the natural things (*Naturursachen*) the causality of which must stand under empirical laws . . . [8] Man, however, who knows all the rest of nature solely through the senses, knows himself also through pure apperception; and this, indeed, in acts and inner determinations which he cannot regard as impressions of the senses. . . (A 546, B 574)

Since it will presently have significance for my discussion, we should note here that one act of inner determination Kant has in mind is signalled by the 'ought' (*das Sollen*) which;

expresses a possible action the ground of which cannot be anything but a mere concept; whereas in the case of a merely natural action the ground must always be an appearance...No matter how many natural grounds or how many sensuous impulses may impel me to will, they can never give rise to the ought, but only to a willing which, while being very far from necessity, is always conditioned; and the ought pronounced by Reason confronts such willing with a limit and an end, yes, forbids or authorizes it. (A 548, B 576)

Here Kant's epistemological dualism between the formal and material elements of cognitive experience, which was subsequently crystallised in the ontological dualism between the phenomenal and noumenal realms, becomes decisive for his philosophical anthropology. In other words, the tension between physical and rational determination becomes constitutive of human nature itself. The resultant picture is in keeping with one which has dotted the pages of Occidental philosophy since Plato first assigned man an intermediate position between the realms of being and becoming, the eternal and the temporal: humanity as a form of existence torn between the claims of the flesh and the dictates of the mind. To succumb to the former is to remain as a dumb brute, in Kant's formulation a will determined or constituted only through pathological or sensuous motives is purely animal (*arbitrium brutum*).(A 802, B 830) But through the Word - in Kant's formulation, the 'ought' expressed by Reason – the strictures of physical nature can be overcome and our uniqueness as rational and free beings affirmed.[9]

Read as an attempt to reconcile the break between the phenomenal and noumenal realms, by focussing upon human beings as subjects whose actions can alternately be considered the result of a free or a natural causality, Kant's solution to the Third Antinomy of Pure Reason is not wholly compatible with the central teachings of the first *Critique*. As with so much of the discussion of freedom in this study, it is difficult to avoid the impression that Kant is here preparing the ground for the *Critique of Practical Reason* rather than establishing our knowledge of freedom within the conditions of the first *Critique*. Specifically, there is no ground for the implication that man's knowledge of himself through pure apperception, and in inner states and determinations, constitutes *theoretical* knowledge of the noumenal realm and/or the transcendental idea of freedom. While it is the case that the first *Critique* establishes our ability to know ourselves without reference to objects in space, and thereby validates the legitimacy of a pure self-consciousness, this knowledge is not entirely free of the conditions of sensibility. On the contrary, such knowledge is still subject to the condition of time, and 'while time is not an empirical concept that has been derived from any experience', (B 46) it is most definitely a condition of sensibility. (B 54) Thus, knowledge of *the self* is still a contingent knowledge, rather than knowledge of a transcendental idea which, by definition, must stand beyond the conditioning of time as well as that of space.

At least one Kant-scholar carries this point one step further to declare that 'the experience of moral obligation – which Kant called the one fact of Pure Reason – occurs in time, in inner sense, and therefore involves sensible intuition'.[10] Admittedly, there is a problem when one tries to speak of an experience beyond time. However, I disagree with John Silber's further assertion that we might help Kant out of this dilemma by broadening the conception of the phenomenal world to include all aspects of human experience – the moral, aesthetic, and organic, no less than the theoretical. . .[11] Such an approach would undermine most of the intended consequences of the *Critique of Pure Reason*, particularly the limits which that work seeks to impose upon the claims and possibilities of scientific understanding. I will argue, subsequently, that rather than expand Kant's conception of sensible experience to embrace moral experience, we should recognise that the latter signifies a qualitatively different mode of experience.

To some degree it would be misleading to belabour this point, since Kant himself goes on to deny that his solution to the Third Antinomy contains a demonstration of freedom.

> It has not been our intention to prove the possibility of freedom. For in this also we should not have succeeded, since we cannot from mere concepts *a priori* know the possibility of any real ground and its causality. . . What we have been able to show, and what we have alone been concerned to show, is that this antinomy rests on a sheer illusion, and that causality through freedom is at least *not incompatible with nature*. (A 558, B 586)

With this disclaimer, Kant returns to his former position in which the contrary notions of a free and a natural causality might each be sustained only by maintaining a rigid dualism between the phenomenal and noumenal realms. And yet, as I have suggested, it is difficult to ignore the extent to which the discussion of freedom here anticipates the more systematic treatment to come in the *Critique of Practical Reason*. It is difficult, in other words, to believe that Kant never intends to provide intimations of a solution to the problem of freedom in the present work. His characterisation of human nature as a nature in tension between two sources of determination, and the significance he attaches to our capacity to confront the dictates of our senses with limits which are wholly rational in their origins, would have to be read as a digression if we were to accept his contention that all he intends to show is the possible compatibility of spontaneous and natural causality. But that discussion is too finely drawn, and the position it occupies in his analysis too central, to be read as a diversion.

Moreover, the theme of the ought and the bifurcated image of human nature are not momentary concerns with Kant. Again, their appearance in the first *Critique* prefigures the course which his later resolution of the problem of freedom will follow. Hence, it seems to me that in his solution to the Third Antinomy Kant begins to reach for a demonstration of freedom only to realise that he is threatening the limits which a critical account of theoretical, empirical, and scientific understanding must impose upon the capacity of such modes of cognition to explicate the nature of the transcendental. In moving beyond experience to speculate on the nature of the noumenal realm, Kant is abridging those conditions that would allow him to demonstrate the reality of whatever concepts his thought might encounter within that realm. For it is a fundamental tenet of the *Critique of Pure Reason* that such demonstrations can occur only *in* experience, understood as the *empirical knowledge of appearances*.

SUMMARY

With this last observation we have managed to highlight the most obvious implications of Kant's first critical work for his ethics. We have seen that within the context of his dualism, morality is only possible if human beings are in some sense free of that all pervasive determination which characterises the empirical, or phenomenal, domain of being. Secondly, we have seen that the possible liberation of humans from this domain must depend upon philosophy, namely with Reason's ability and need to establish the concept of a causality that stands beyond all natural determination: the concept of a transcendental freedom. And, finally, we have seen that so long as experience is equated with the knowledge of objects in space and time, that is, with the empirical knowledge of appearances, freedom remains inaccessible. Only through a radical shift in perspective is Kant able to think *concretely* of freedom, and thereby establish that absolute and pure foundation for the moral will which his ethics demands. This shift is signalled in his move from the philosophical investigation of thought in its theoretical employment (*The Critique of Pure Reason*) to a similarly systematic exploration of thought in its practical employment (*The Critique of Practical Reason*).

2
The Formal Ethics

A NOTE ON METHOD

Despite the thematic difference between Kant's first and second *Critiques* they share one important feature: in both studies he rigidly adheres to the transcendental method of deduction. The following citation from Norman Kemp Smith serves as a particularly clear depiction of that method as well as an indication of its role in the *Critique of Practical Reason*.

> The moral law, though a form of pure Reason, exercises in the process of its transcendental proof, a function which exactly corresponds to that which is discharged by possible experience in the first *Critique*. Our consciousness of the moral law is, like sense-experience, a given fact. It is *de facto* and cannot be deduced from anything more ultimate than itself. But as given, it enables us to deduce its transcendental conditions. This does not mean that our immediate consciousness of it *as given* guarantees its validity. The nature of its validity is established only in the process whereby it reveals its necessary implications.[1]

In keeping with this symmetry, my concern in the present chapter will be to identify and explicate the implications of the moral law in a manner similar to the foregoing discussion of Kant's analysis of sense-experience. But, whereas the ethical significance of sense-experience was largely negative, insofar as it served to 'protect' the idea of freedom from the determinism which pervades scientific and empirical knowledge, we shall see that as Kant reflects on the meaning of what is entailed in our consciousness of the moral law he strives to affirm the reality of a decisively different realm of human experience and understanding.

THE MORAL LAW AND ITS FOUNDATION IN FREEDOM

The moral law or categorical imperative – 'act always so that the maxim of thy will can at the same time be considered as a principle of universal legislation' – signifies, for Kant, the ability of a rational creature to transform a subjective principle of its will (a principle grounded in its particular desires and intentions) into an objective law which would be binding for the will of *any* rational being. It is impossible to exaggerate the importance of this capacity for Kant. For, when he writes that the formulation of the moral law 'puts the will into a realm totally different from the empirical',[2] he is, in effect, claiming to have established that foothold among the transcendental ideas that thought, in its theoretical employment, was unable to secure. The moral law is nothing more nor less than a transcendental fact (that is, a 'rational' proposition) and by making it the point of departure for the second *Critique* Kant serves clear notice that Reason is at last manoeuvring on its home territory and playing the game according to its own rules.

The first condition which our consciousness of the moral law implies is the ability to conceive of a will that is independent of all material conditioning or, in the language of the first *Critique*, one which is free of natural causality. 'It is therefore the moral law, of which we become directly conscious. . . that first presents itself to us, and leads directly to the concept of freedom, since Reason presents it as a principle of determination which can be outweighed by sensible conditions, yes, which is wholly independent of them'.[3] It might seem that this is the same negative formulation of freedom we discussed in the previous chapter. But in fact, the presence of the moral law makes it possible here for Kant to speak concretely of a causality that can function in independence from those conditions imposed upon our actions by natural circumstances. There is no need to complicate his intention. His point is that in becoming conscious of the moral law, we become aware that regardless of any empirical motives that might compel us to act in a certain manner, we can always pause and test the maxim of that action by universalising it in accord with the formula of this law. And, against this universal law we can judge the morality of our proposed act, that is, determine whether or not we *ought* to carry it through in practice.

The crucial feature of this development is that through the practical exercise of Reason – 'practical', in the sense that Reason is here informing and guiding practice – we have determined ourselves to act or not to act; in other words, we have exercised causality in exemption from the imperatives of the empirical world. Here then is the idea of freedom, not simply as a speculative and ultimately inscrutable hypothesis, but as the *a priori* ground of the moral law.

With this brief paraphrase I have deliberately cast Kant's position in the most favourable light possible. As I have stated it, his case has a distinct ring of common sense for we are, in many instances at least, able to so generalise the justifications for our projected deeds and, as Kant would have it, this possibility bears the distinct mark of an intellectual freedom. But with this, we cannot conclude that his transcendental deduction of freedom is beyond question. As Kant hastens to acknowledge, it appears as though he is postulating the moral law to verify the reality of freedom and subsequently calling forth the said freedom to establish the legitimacy of the moral law.

Kant's response to this anticipated objection is his insistence that the respective functions of these two 'moments' of freedom are altogether different. Within his scheme of reference, our ability to conceive of the moral law leads us to consider the *possibility* of freedom (the moral law is the *ratio cognoscendi* of freedom) while the *reality* of freedom thereby disclosed to us serves to sustain (as a *ratio essendi*) the moral law.[4]

The distinction Kant is making here is in accord with the interpretation of Norman Kemp Smith cited above. Kant begins with the moral law as an object or datum of consciousness, but he cannot explain and verify its validity for us until he has disclosed the condition which makes it possible, namely, freedom.

Structurally, then, Kant's demonstration of freedom is a thoroughly consistent application of the transcendental method of deduction. And there can be no doubt that with this deduction of freedom, Kant has taken a significant step beyond the discussions of causality through freedom and morality of the first *Critique*. Indeed, if we consider this present development as a stage in the evolution of his philosophy it is not, I think, inappropriate to characterise it as his personal act of liberation. Here he is finally free of the strictures and demands imposed upon his thoughts by the concern to critique the premises and possibilities of empirical knowledge. We have an indication of the relief he must have enjoyed, with his comment that compared with the labours of the first *Critique* the work which followed would be an amusement. (A xii) However, Kant is not at liberty to stray from the foundations laid down in that earlier work. No matter how high his intellectual edifice might eventually soar it must still conform to the geometry of its base: it must still adhere to the dualism between a phenomenal realm of empirical nature and a noumenal realm of intelligible being.

There are ample indications throughout his later work that Kant recognised this; one of the first we find in the second *Critique* occurs during his discussion of the will.

WILLE AND *WILLKÜR*: THE TWO MOMENTS OF FREEDOM

One of Kant's most subtle and perplexing distinctions is that which he draws between the pure will (*Wille*) which can only be determined by the legislative *form* of the maxim and the pathologically effected or 'elective' will (*Willkür*) that is influenced by subjective and material considerations.[5] The presence here of the familiar juxtaposition between form and matter correctly implies that the distinction between *Wille* and *Willkür* is yet another manifestation of the phenomenal-noumenal dichotomy. However, this expression of the dichotomy is considerably softer than the ones we encountered in the *Critique of Pure Reason*. Whereas there he asserted that, as a phenomenal entity, man must be seen as subject to the law of natural causality, he now claims that the pathologically effected will is not wholly determined by empirical conditions. '. . . 'eine pathologisch affizierte (obgleich dadurch nicht bestimmte, mithin auch immer freie) Willkür'. . .[6] Kant's desire to reserve some residue of freedom for the empirically conditioned will is, I suggest, an attempt to obviate a problem present from the first pages of the second *Critique*.

We have noted his contention that the articulation of the moral law signals a movement whereby the will transcends the phenomenal realm towards the noumenal. Kant can justify this occurrence only by insisting that, despite the influences exerted upon it by virtue of its phenomenal character, the will is in some sense free. For the initial recognition of the possibility of freedom, that is, the move *towards* the noumenal realm, is one which must occur *within* the phenomenal realm. We can describe this circumstance in terms of the following paradox: the will, or man as a willful actor, must *be* free in order to *become* free.

One possible way of resolving this problem is to read Kant's distinction between *Wille* and *Willkür* as his attempt to distinguish, for purposes of analysis, between two functions or 'parts' of a single and unitary faculty, a distinction of the same order as that between Reason and Understanding. This is the interpretation favoured by John Silber,[7] and is apparently supported by Kant's definition of the autonomy and heteronomy of the will as well as the distinction Kant draws between a positive and a negative 'moment' of freedom.

> the autonomy of the will (*Willen*) is the sole principle of all moral laws and of all duties which conform to them; all heteronomy of the will (*Willkür*) is, on the contrary, not at all grounded in any obligation, but is opposed to this principle and to the morality of the will. The sole principle of morality consists in the independence of the law from all material (namely, a desired [object] and at the same time in the determination of the will (*Willkür*) through the mere legislative form of which its maxim is capable. This independence is freedom in the negative sense; this self-legislation of the pure, and as such practical, Reason is freedom in the positive sense. Thus the moral law expresses nothing else than the autonomy of pure practical Reason, that is, freedom; and this is itself the formal condition of all maxims and it is only under this condition that they can agree with the supreme practical law.[8]

Here, despite his use of the alternative expressions *Wille* and *Willkür*, Kant seems to be saying that the same will is both autonomous and heteronomous. In recognising its heteronomy Kant is, according to Silber's interpretation, acknowledging the obvious fact that '. . . moral volition is ineluctably temporal. The will is tempted in time, and, depending on its decision, feels guilty or satisfied in time'.[9] To be sure, as heteronomous, *Willkür* can choose between ends that are subjective and in so doing is determined by the principle of private happiness (*eigenen Glückseligkeit*). But, again following Silber's reading, *Willkür* is also autonomous and may elect to determine its actions objectively in compliance with the moral law.[10] In so doing it would be bringing itself under the authority of the pure will (*Wille*) which, according to Silber, 'is not free at all. *Wille* is rather the law of freedom, the normative aspect of the will, which as a norm is under no constraint or pressure. It exerts, instead, the pressure of its own normative rational nature upon *Willkür*'.[11]

Silber's is a concerted attempt to resolve the problem we first observed in chapter 1; namely the question of how a wholly rational freedom can exercise causality in time. For Silber is correct in stating that 'as long as the acts of moral volition cannot alter the determination of events in the phenomenal world, all categorical demands that they do so are in vain'.[12] What is more, his attention to the normative character of the idea of freedom (and its corollary, the concept of a pure will) highlights an important feature of Kant's ethics that we will subsequently consider in more detail. Ultimately, however, Silber's reading of Kant is inconsistent with Silber's own initial premises and reaches too far beyond the letter of Kant's position.

By ascribing the activity of freedom only to *Willkür*, Silber jeopardises his earlier contention that *Wille* and *Willkür* are two elements of the same faculty. If *Wille* is simply a norm and is, in itself, 'neither free nor unfree', then it has no capacity to initiate action and no ability to exercise an autonomously authoritative function. In short, it does not have the characteristics that Kant ascribes to a faculty. Silber's claim, then, contradicts Kant's contention that *Wille* is autonomous and that this autonomy expresses the capacity of *pure practical Reason* to direct and determine the activity of the heteronomous will (*Willkür*) in accordance with the moral law. Kant's definition expressly states that, as autonomous, the pure will is (negatively) free *from* material determination and (positively) free *to* determine itself formally.

Thus, as I read Kant, he is insisting that there are two 'moments' of freedom and two corresponding aspects of the will. The negative moment of freedom expresses the capacity of *Willkür* to overcome the desires, motives, and determinations of the phenomenal world, as well as the potential to translate the maxims of such intentions and bases into a universal and legislative form. The positive moment of freedom, on the other hand, expresses the capacity of Reason, in its practical employment, to articulate this formal condition as a moral law or categorical imperative, thereby signalling the ability of the *Wille* to constrain the pathological and heteronomous will through what Kant suggests 'may be called an internal, but intellectual compulsion'.[13] Only, then, if we recognise that *Wille* and *Willkür* designate, as Silber originally contends, two dimensions of a unitary faculty, can we agree with Kant's assertion that the situation he is describing is one that reveals the will as a self-determining faculty. The fact that Silber has strayed far from this initial insight is most evident in his conclusion.

From the moment he assigns all responsibility for freedom to *Willkür*, Silber begins to break down the elemental Kantian distinction between the phenomenal and noumenal realms. For we have seen that Kant wants to designate, with *Willkür*, a relation of the will to the phenomenal world. When one asserts, as does Silber, that this dimension of the will is autonomous, as well as heteronomous, then one is forced to broaden 'the conception of the phenomenal world to include all aspects of human experience – the moral, aesthetic, and organic, no less than the theoretical'.[14] Silber's consequent reduction of *Wille* to a wholly passive role entails a corresponding devaluation of the significance of the noumenal realm in Kant's philosophy. To his credit, Silber does not fail to acknowledge as much. But, when he concludes that his analysis will 'pose many tasks for Kant's interpreters, but no insurmountable problems for Kant's system',[15] I cannot concur. For without the distinction between phenomenal and noumenal, as designations of two distinctive modes of existence, Kant's critique of theoretical Reason would collapse, his Copernican Revolution would be vitiated, and freedom would cease to be a function of pure practical Reason. What is more, the thrust of the Kantian ethic is not towards the extension of the phenomenal realm that Silber describes, but, as I will argue below, involves an expansion of the noumenal or intelligible realm and a *diminution* of the significance of the phenomenal realm.

THE INTELLIGIBLE WORLD

With the preceding discussion I have not intended to suggest that the problems addressed in Silber's essay can be resolved by a mere reiteration or paraphrasing of Kant's distinctions and definitions. If anything, the difficulties in which Silber's interpretation becomes entangled only serve to highlight the complexities of Kant's moral philosophy. For the transcendental deduction of freedom has clearly placed freedom within the noumenal realm, beyond time, and thereby rendered the prospects of ever contemplating anything 'happening' through freedom, suspect. And yet we must do so, because the image that Kant presents us is clearly that of a process: the determination of the will by the purified form of its maxim, as well as the negative and positive moments of freedom, must be conceived of as events. Faced with this dilemma, there is a great temptation to despair and abandon all hope of finding our way through the Kantian labyrinth. But against this impulse, we must weigh the fact that Kant is not speaking nonsense. As I have already indicated in the previous chapter, the situation he describes accurately reflects an important feature of our moral experience. The capacity to confront private claims with the idea of generalisable goods and public duties is, if not the exclusive mark of morality, as Kant might have it, nonetheless, one important indication that a moral consciousness is at work. For this reason alone, we are obliged to pursue his intentions. And, to this end, we are aided by the fact that Kant appreciated the difficulties of his formulations and was continually re-casting his reflections to explain how 'pure Reason can be practical, that is, can in itself determine the will independently of anything empirical'.[16] In the context of one such attempt – 'The Deduction of the Fundamental Principles of Pure Practical Reason' – his thought takes a turn which, I will maintain, points the way towards a resolution markedly different from any we have yet encountered.

We have already noted the importance of the moral law as Kant's point of departure for the move from the phenomenal to the noumenal realms. But, once he feels secure with his reflections on the latter, he does not rest with the 'discovery' of freedom and the proclamation of the will's autonomy as the sole principle of all moral laws. Rather, while he continues to maintain that the idea of freedom is the only thing that we can *know* of the intelligible world, he argues that we can legitimately conceive of an intelligible system of Nature (*eine Natur unter der Autonomie der reiner praktischen Vernunft*) that is analogous to the sensible world (*die Natur der Sinneswelt*). Obviously, this claim is more ambitious than any we have yet considered. Kant's thoughts in this regard are, therefore, worth presenting in some detail.

Now, a system of Nature, in the most general sense, is the existence of things under laws. The sensible nature of rational beings in general is their existence under laws empirically conditioned, which, from the point of view of Reason, is *heteronomy*. The supersensible (*die übersinnliche*) nature of the same beings, on the other hand, is their existence according to laws which are independent on every empirical condition, and therefore belong to the *autonomy* of pure Reason. And, since the laws by which the existence of things depends on cognition are practical, supersensible nature, so far as we can form any notion of it, is nothing else than *a system of Nature under the autonomy of pure practical Reason*. Now, the law of this autonomy is the moral law, which, therefore, is the fundamental law of a supersensible nature, and of a pure world of understanding (*einer reinen Verstandeswelt*), whose counterpart must exist in the world of sense, but without interfering with its laws. We might call the former the *archetypal* world (*natura archetypa*), which we know only in the Reason, and the latter the *ectypal* world (*natura ectypa*), because it contains the possible effect of the idea of the former which is the determining principle of the will.[17]

Here is the crowning expression of Kant's dualism: two independent but parallel worlds, each with its own system of *a priori* laws. The first, a world of objects in space and time conditioned by the demands of empirical knowledge; the second, a world of purely intelligible being grounded in the cognition of the moral law. The two worlds co-exist in the species Man, insofar as humans are rational subjects, but these domains cannot and must not coincide: the laws of supersensible Nature must not interfere with the laws of the empirical world.

This last observation should dispel any doubt that Kant is prepared to sacrifice the achievements of the first *Critique* to accomplish his goals in the second. Indeed, as his argument proceeds his concern for the ability of the free will to exercise causality in time – that is, to initiate a series of events within the empirical world – appears to diminish. Instead, Kant's attention now turns to the role of freedom *within* the intelligible world, rather than with the ability of the free will to determine events in the phenomenal world. He even goes so far as to explicitly disclaim any concern with the latter possibility.

It is left to the theoretic principles of Reason to decide whether the causality of the will suffices for the realization of the objects or not, this being an inquiry into the possibility of objects of volition. Intuition of these objects is therefore of no importance to the practical problem. We are here concerned only with the determination of the will and the determining principles of its maxims as a free will, not at all with the result. For, provided only that the *will* conforms to the law of pure reason, then let its power in execution be what it may . . . , this is no concern of the critique, which only inquires whether, and in what way, pure reason can be practical, that is directly determine the will.[18]

EFFICIENT AND FORMAL CAUSALITY

We would be in error to conclude from the preceding remarks that Kant has abandoned his search for some principle or concept which would allow him to speak of an interaction between the noumenal and phenomenal realms. As his elaboration of the supersensible system of Nature indicates, Kant continues to maintain that laws constituted by pure practical Reason can have 'effect' in the sensible world. However, it does seem that Kant is moving away from his earlier attempts to describe the causality exercised by the moral law in the terms of an efficient model of causality, that is, to affirm the capacity of freedom spontaneously to initiate a series of temporal events. A more accurate account of what is occurring at this stage of his critique must consider the possibility that he is being forced into adopting a modified conception of freedom.

We have seen repeatedly, most recently in our discussion of the will, the contradictions involved in attempting to ascribe efficient causality to freedom: such a formulation requires that the agency of freedom stand, even if only for some action-spawning moment, within time. But, the difficulty is resolved – if not mitigated altogether – if we consider the causality of freedom in formal, rather than efficient, terms. For Aristotle's initial definition of formal causality specifically allows for a principle of movement and change that is itself beyond the determination of time.

. . .the form or the archetype, i.e., the statement of the essence and its genera, are called 'causes'. . . Now the principles which cause motion in a physical way are two, *of which one is not physical*, as it has no principle of motion in itself. Of this kind is whatever causes movement, not being itself moved, such as (1) that which is completely unchangeable, the primary reality, and (2) the essence of that which is coming to be, i.e., the form; for this is the end or 'that for the sake of which'.[19] (my emphasis).

We have seen indications, in Silber's highlighting of the normative character of *der Wille* and Kant's characterisation of the intelligible world as 'archetypal', that Kant's notions of freedom and the autonomous will might answer these Aristotelean criteria. Moreover, we have noted an unmistakable tendency in Kant to point towards the autonomous use of Reason as an expression of Man's essential nature. But, while these features may encourage the interpretation I am advancing here, they hardly constitute a definitive case for its validity. Before we can say with any degree of certainty that Kant is indeed turning towards a formal or final notion of causality, we need to better comprehend the role freedom plays within the intelligible realm and to better appreciate the influence that realm exerts upon humans insofar as we are sensuous creatures.

MORAL EXPERIENCE

In his discussion of the 'Typic' of pure practical judgement Kant defines the criteria which any explication of the intelligible order must meet. We can speak safely, he writes, only of those intelligible objects 'to which Reason might lead us in following the guidance of this (moral) law', and these intelligible objects 'can have no reality for us than to serve the purpose of this law and the employment of practical Reason'.[20] Once again, we are reminded of the crucial role the moral law plays in Kantian philosophy. Without it, Reason is condemned to flounder aimlessly in a sea of transcendent and chimerical ideas; with its guidance, Reason can embark with confidence upon a voyage to a whole new realm of experience. And the remainder of the second *Critique* is precisely this; the disclosure of a moral experience that differs as greatly from the experience which characterised the phenomenal realm as the idea of freedom differs from the law of natural causality. For example, before the second *Critique* is concluded Kant will speak affirmatively of love and happiness, two states of emotion he has previously ruled outside the bounds of moral significance because of their relationship to the conditions of privacy and subjectivity. But now, predictably, the source and object of such emotions is purely intellectual: happiness describes that state of contentment induced by the contemplation of our freedom, while love is that *practical* love expressed in the commandment to love God above everything else and our neighbours as ourselves.[21] However, the dominant emotion of our moral experience is, for Kant, respect (*Achtung*).

Despite the fact that no subjective motive can be allowed morally to determine or influence the will, the converse does not hold: there is at least one instance in which we must necessarily presume that our feelings are affected by the moral law.

> . . . the moral law, as a determining principle of the will, must through the thwarting of all our inclinations, produce a feeling which may be called pain. Here we have the first, perhaps the only, instance in which we are able from *a priori* considerations to determine the relation of a cognition (in this case of pure practical Reason) to the feeling of pleasure or displeasure.[22]

To be sure, this is an entirely negative effect, but Kant wants to claim that it has positive significance. For, while our initial feeling may be one of pain, we must, upon further reflection, pay tribute to the purely formal principle which is able to oppose and humble the merely physical propensities of our nature. We must, in other words, come to recognise that insofar as it is something positive in itself and able to suppress (*niederschlägen*) our self-conceit, the moral law 'is the ground of a positive feeling that is not empirical and is known *a priori*. Thus, respect for the moral law is a feeling which we can know completely *a priori* and whose necessity we can comprehend'.[23]

There is a wide spectrum of possible reactions to these claims. At one extreme we should not fail to note the presence here of an authoritarian streak in Kant's ethics, an authoritarianism whose oppressiveness is only partially diminished by the knowledge that he is describing the tyranny of Reason. For example, in his

Phenomenology of Spirit, Hegel brilliantly exposed the malevolent dialectic whereby the unchecked authority of pure and absolute freedom translates into the practice of a terror every bit as awesome as any totalitarianism ever mounted in the name of the irrational.[24]

A somewhat less severe consideration is whether Kant is too arbitrary with his selection of 'respect' as that feeling most characteristic of moral experience. Might not 'fear' or 'anxiety', for example, more accurately depict the situation he describes? Any attempt to give an exhaustive response to these concerns would carry us far beyond the scope of this study. But we can acknowledge that Kant employs the attitude of respect with a definite purpose in mind, and that he makes a considerable effort to defend his contention that with this he is describing a feeling which can be known in an *a priori* manner.

From the very outset of his post-critical ethical writings (that is, with the *Fundamental Principles of the Metaphysics of Morals*), Kant maintains that goodness does not simply typify action in accord with the moral law but, rather, signifies only that action taken *for the sake* of the moral law. We can summarise his many expressions of this theme by noting that the moral individual will not be one whose actions simply conform *with* the moral law (the motive in this case might well be a desire to enhance one's material circumstances or avoid punishment), but he who acts *because of* the moral law; that is, the individual who knows the true nature and source of morality and acts solely on the basis of that knowledge. Leaving aside the somewhat troubling implication that, with this condition, Kant seems to be restricting the field of ethical practice to students of philosophy, the important feature for our discussion here is that, with this doctrine, Kant is committing himself to the view that the motivation of the will is the governing element in our determinations of the good act and the ethical actor.

But, even the purest of motives is tinged with some degree of subjectivity and feeling, a fact Kant is genuinely aware of in the passages we are now considering. His problem, then, is to describe a feeling that will provide a motive to ethical action without compromising the purity of the moral will. It is in this context that we must read his choice and definition of respect as that feeling which, despite sharing in the condition of sensibility which is the ground of all feelings, is nonetheless objective insofar as it has its cause (*Ursache*) in the realm of pure practical Reason.[25]

Is this, at last, an instance of practical Reason exercising efficient causality within the empirical or 'sensible' realm? While much of Kant's discussion would seem to suggest an affirmative answer, close study of his argument and the ensuing discussion will not support such a reading. For whenever Kant describes the immediate effects of the moral law upon sensibility he speaks in terms of negative dispositions – of pain, displeasure, and humiliation (*Demütigung*) – which do not accord with his characterisation of respect as a 'positive' feeling. More significantly, as he refines his definition of respect he emphasises its 'indirect' influence upon sensibility.

> Respect for the moral law, then, must be regarded as a positive, though indirect, effect of it on feeling, inasmuch as this respect weakens the impeding influence of inclinations by humiliating self-esteem; and hence also as a subjective principle of activity, that is, as a *motive* to obedience to the law, and as a principle of the maxims of a life conformable to it.[26]

Whether this statement represents a modification of Kant's earlier definition, or simply a more detailed elaboration is not too important here. What is significant is the fact that once again we find him bowing before the disjunction between the intelligible and empirical worlds. Either respect is a necessary and universal implication of the moral law or it has its source in the emotions. In the former case, respect enjoys the status of an *a priori* condition of practical Reason and has immediate relevance only within the intelligible world; in the latter case it is a physical phenomenon and cannot, by definition, be categorised as *a priori*. Kant chooses to preserve the *a priori* character of respect and thus concludes by describing a feeling that can only have indirect bearing upon our sentient natures, which is devoid of all material content, and which 'cannot be reckoned as either pleasure or pain'.[27] In brief, he ends these reflections on the nature of respect by describing a feeling which, by all normal accounts, is not a feeling but, rather, a formal principle in precisely the same sense, and to the same extent, as the transcendental ideas of freedom and the moral will.

There is, in my judgement, only one manner in which Kant can maintain that respect for the moral law denotes subjectivity. This has nothing to do with man as a *sentient* creature but, on the contrary, refers to humans as members (or subjects) of the intelligible world. We have already seen that respect is provoked by (and is the just desert of) that individual who acts only for the sake of the moral law. And we know, further, that the capacity to act in such a manner designates, for Kant, our rational, as opposed to our phenomenal, nature. Thus, to the extent that we act out of respect for the moral law we are not to be considered as sentient creatures but as 'legislative members of a moral kingdom rendered possible by freedom and presented to us by reason as an object of respect. . .'[28]

The notion of humans as members of a moral kingdom is, of course, not new with the second *Critique*. Earlier, in the *Fundamental Principles*, Kant writes of Man as a member of a kingdom of ends.[29] But that earlier formulation remained hypothetical and tentative, lacking the secure foundation supplied only through the transcendental deduction of freedom. Here, with the reality of freedom established, as well as the attendant conception of an intelligible world, Kant is able to explore the full implications of his insight. As he does so he further testifies to the severe distinction between man's rational and sentient nature by introducing a new conception to designate the former, namely, the concept of personality.

PERSONALITY AND THE PERSON

On at least one occasion in his analysis of respect, Kant states that 'respect applies only to persons, not to things'.[30] While his intention at that point is to mark the general distinction between human beings and the other objects of physical nature, his use of the term 'person' in this context is telling insofar as it indicates that the term will denote our moral capacity. Subsequently, Kant develops this theme in more detail.

> Personality is freedom and independence from the mechanism of nature, yet considered at the same time as the capacity (*Vermögen*) of a being which has a peculiar characteristic, namely, from its own Reason it gives itself pure practical laws, so that the person as a member of the sensible world is subject to its own personality, insofar as it belongs to the intelligible world; it is, then, not surprising that man, as a member of both

worlds, must consider his own essence (*Wesen*), with regard to this second and highest definition, with nothing but reverence, and his own laws with the highest respect.[31]

This is the most explicit expression yet of a point intimated throughout this chapter, namely, that the elemental nature of humans does not lie simply in their rational capacity but is, rather, to be found in a specific application of Reason. With Kant, 'Man' designates not merely the rational species, more crucially, it designates the moral species. Reason, to the extent that it is no longer subordinated to the demands of finite experience, ultimately comes into its own as *practical* Reason. By the same token, our essence is not expressed in the capacity to lend our understanding to the demands of sense experience and empirical knowledge. In such instances, Reason becomes a utilitarian means for the achievement of ends that lie beyond the core of our humanity. And we become, in a sense, contingent upon the conditions such ends impose. Conversely, the only essential relationships into which Reason – and man as a rational being – can enter, are those in which it is not contingent upon any external conditions but, rather, is completely autonomous, that is, subject to conditions of its own making. This is the meaning of Kant's assertion that Man's essence is expressed in his personality. It is, further, the intent of Kant's subsequent claim that, as Person, Man must be considered an end in himself.[32]

The elemental morality of human beings is not the only point that becomes explicit in this conception of personality. Earlier we saw that Kant describes the relationship of the intelligible world to the phenomenal as 'archetypal'. Now, as he comments on the exemplary character of personality, Kant provides a helpful illustration of his intent. To witness the life of a Person is, he writes, to be confronted with an instance (*Beispiel*) of the moral law, an instance that stands as either a reproach or an exemplar for the conduct of our own lives, and which must necessarily command our respect.[33] The obvious allusion here is to those exemplary figures whose lives are governed by the moral law and who thereby testify to the efficacy of that law: those individuals who serve as models for what others can and should become, namely Persons.

A somewhat less obvious feature of this claim is that it presupposes the notion of the individual as a subject in a moral 'kingdom', as well as the indivisibility of that kingdom. I cannot experience the presence of personality in the other as an exhortation, unless I share in the capacity for moral self-determination which personality signifies. And Kant cannot argue that the life of a Person *must* command our respect unless all individuals are capable of becoming Persons. Just as we all share in the practical capacity of Reason, so too we all share in the promise of personality. Thus, the concept of man as a moral subject and the notion of personality coincide, with the result that the intelligible world, insofar as it is a world of moral subjects, becomes for Kant, 'a world of personalities'.[34]

To this point Kant has preserved the distinction between the moral law, taken as the immediate datum of moral experience, and those concepts – freedom, the will and personality – that are the universal and necessary postulates of that lawful experience. However, in one of his last discourses on morality Kant explicitly identifies the moral law with personality. 'We cannot rightly call the idea of the moral law, with the respect which is inseparable from it, a *predisposition* to *personality*; it is personality itself (the idea of humanity considered quite intellectually).'[35]

Here we see that Kant's thought has come full circle: he began with the moral law as an irreducible fact of consciousness and pursued its implications to disclose the cognitive reality of freedom together with the autonomous will, two themes that converge in the concept of personality. Now this concept appears to collapse back into the notion of the moral law. But we ought not conclude, therefrom, that Kant's reflections are merely the spinning out of a tautology. On the contrary, there is a qualitative difference between the moral law that his thoughts began with and the moral law to which he now refers. The former was simply a formal proposition, at best a standard against which he could plot and validate the progress of practical Reason. However, in its last and complete expression, the term is laden with the meaning this progress has disclosed; Kant's identification of the moral law with personality is, in my judgement, intended to signal the fact that the moral law is not simply the touchstone, but the consummation, of practical Reason.

In a critical way, then, the difference between the moral law that serves as the point of departure for Kant's analysis and the moral law which comes to be identified with personality, is analogous to the contrast between some feature of the world which presents itself to the senses unanalysed and that same feature after it has been reflected upon and raised to the level of theoretical understanding. Except, that in this case we have to add that the process by which that understanding is achieved is definitive for a specific function of Reason. When Reason deduces the necessary relationship between the moral law and personality, it demonstrates its practical capacity, that is, its capacity to make a purely formal rule (the moral law) a regulative principle for a subject (the Person).

THE ETHICAL SIGNIFICANCE OF PERSONALITY

As the rather fragmentary nature of this discussion has indicated, Kant's conception of personality is neither as fully developed nor as central to his ethics as the concepts of freedom, the will, and the intelligible world. It seems appropriate, then, to provide some explanation of my concern with this relatively minor theme in a survey which, because of its brevity, might be expected to touch only the main points of Kant's analysis.

One reason for devoting some attention to Kant's treatment of personality is that its absence would leave us unaware of one of the greatest insights of modern ethics. Briefly, Kant has asserted that insofar as an individual is conceived of as a Person – that is, as an autonomous and rational creature – he or she must command our respect. Further, as such a creature, he or she can never be treated as an object or as a means for the achievement of some end beyond his or her self: as Person, the individual human being is an end in itself. To treat the Person as an object would be to subject him or her to the laws of physical nature alone, laws which he or she transcends by virtue of the Person's stature within the intelligible world. To treat the other as an object or a means is nothing less, then, than a violation of his or her essential humanity. We can carry this crucial insight further and note that individuals who use others as a means are themselves debased. The aspects of Person and personality are universal and necessary attributes of *any* and *all* rational beings. To deny or violate them in one instance is to abrogate their universality and, by implication, to deny them in every instance; just as a single abrogation of the laws of sentient experience would throw the whole of such experience into chaos.

A second motive for my concern with Kant's theory of personality is that despite the somewhat cursory character of his analysis, its presence in the second *Critique* serves as a welcome antidote to the ethereal quality which pervades the rest of his ethics. In his prior discussion he presents the moral will and freedom as necessary attributes of the *idea* of a rational being, for the most part deliberately avoiding any references to the concrete human being. No doubt this formulation is wholly consistent with the transcendental method of deduction. But, it is exceedingly abstract and, while pure abstraction has its own virtues – in the treatises of metaphysics and mathematics, for example – its presence is disconcerting when we are dealing with matters of existential import; such as the possibilities, conflicts and challenges of the moral life. (This fact could hardly have escaped Kant himself, whose lectures on ethics were so lively and provocative that they often moved many of his students to tears.[36]) Now, with his discussion of personality, we are reminded that the significance of the themes and arguments he ponders and develops throughout the post-critical ethical studies is, in the final analysis, immediate and telling. To be sure, in the strictest sense, the will and freedom remain the objects of a transcendental deduction achieved within the image of a purely rational being. But, with his discussion of personality and the Person, Kant affirms the need to certify that, in a crucial measure and degree, they must come to be seen as attributes of our concrete humanity.

With this, I do not intend to suggest that the import of personality in Kant is merely stylistic or that his explication is beyond criticism. On the contrary, when we turn our attention to the schematic function of this concept within the Kantian ethic we encounter an entirely different dimension of significance and, eventually, the reappearance of an old problem.

PERSONALITY AND MAN

As we have already seen, the concept of personality hardens the distinction that Kant consistently draws between man's sentient and rational character. Before his discussion of personality it was possible (although, at times, difficult) to read this distinction as a difference in perspective only; to assume that Kant was considering one unitary being (Man) in either a phenomenal or noumenal context. But with the introduction of personality and the concept of the Person, which speaks only to the status of Man within the intelligible realm, the distinction becomes much more stark and Kant's thought takes its irreversible turn in the direction of a transcendental idealism. If Man is, by definition, a being in part subject to the determinations of the phenomenal world, then that individual who, through the affirmation of his or her essential morality becomes a Person – and thereby subject only to the determinations of the intelligible world – becomes more than Man, as Man is defined in the first *Critique*. Just as the Kantian ethic may be characterised as a purgatory, so too may the moment in which the individual recognises and acts upon its obligations before the moral law be described as a moment of conversion.

While it would be misleading to leave the impression that this development is the result of a wholly conscious and deliberate effort by Kant, it would be fallacious to assume that he is unaware that the course of his reflections harbours momentous implications. There are, for example, intimations in the second *Critique* that the expression and fulfillment of our moral nature is no simple event, and that the difference between Man and Person no trivial distinction. Kant tells us here that the act of moral self-determination is accompanied by an elevation (*Erhenbung*), with the clear implication that we are thereby 'carried' from the phenomenal to the noumenal realm. He further enjoins us to recognise that while, as human beings, we are imperfect, as Persons we are holy.[37] But his most revealing observations are reserved for a later work: *Religion Within the Limits of Reason Alone*. Indeed, his comments there are in such marked contrast to his earlier writings (and so infrequently considered in the literature on the Kantian ethic) that they are worth savouring at some length.

> But if a man is to become not merely *legally*, but *morally*, a good man (pleasing to God), that is, a man endowed with virtue in its intelligible character (*virtus noumenon*) and one who, knowing something to be his duty, requires no incentive other than this representation of duty itself, *this* cannot be brought about through gradual *reformation* so long as the basis of the maxims remains impure, but must be effected through a revolution in the man's disposition (a going over to the maxim

of holiness of the disposition). He can become a new man only by a kind of rebirth, as it were a new creation (John III, 5; compare also Genesis I, 2), and a change of heart.[38]

We should not be distracted by the fact that Kant no longer refers to Man's moral nature in terms of personality. If anything, the adoption of the term 'new man' expresses a sharper distinction between sentient and moral nature than did the earlier disjunction between 'personality' and 'man'. For now, Kant is presenting us with an absolute choice between a corrupt *verdorben* and a virtuous nature.

There is no reconciliation possible here except by saying that man is under the necessity of, and is therefore capable of, a revolution in his cast of mind, but only of a gradual reform in his sensuous nature (which places obstacles in the way of the former). That is, if a man reverses, by a single unchangeable decision, that highest ground of his maxims whereby he was an evil man (and thus puts on the new man) [*einen neuen Mensch anzieht*], he is, so far as his principle and cast of mind are concerned, a subject susceptible of goodness. . .[39]

One of the most telling features of this claim is the language within which it is couched. When Kant speaks of the act through which the individual moves from a state of evil to a state of goodness as 'revolutionary', and when he describes the being who emerges from this act as a 'new man', he is finally acknowledging the futility of all attempts to locate, within his frame of reference, some principle or entity that will enable him to mediate between the phenomenal and the noumenal realms. He is, in other words, recognising that the system he has constructed embraces two qualitatively different modes of being and that, consequently, any movement between them will entail a similarly qualitative transformation. The difference between what I have come to call 'sentient Man' and 'moral Man' is as fundamental and exclusive as that between natural causality and causality through freedom.

In my judgement, then, at this point Kant is thrown back into the dilemma he first addressed in his 'Solution to the Third Antinomy of Reason': the quandry which results from the assertion that whatever takes place within the intelligible world presupposes and embodies principles that prevail within that world alone, and cannot have any immediate bearing upon conditions and events in the phenomenal world. Through the employment of the faculty of practical Reason, the individual may effect a revolution in his or her cast of mind and thereby, in Kant's terms, become virtuous. But Kant is quick to assert that Man thereby becomes virtuous only in thought: insofar as the individual is a sentient being he or she remains corrupt, indeed insofar as judgement is clouded by the senses, we can never be certain that our motives are pure.

> He (man) can hope that in the light of the purity of the principle which he has adopted as the supreme maxim of his will. . .to find himself upon the good (though strait) path of continual *progress* from bad to better. For him who penetrates (*durchschaut*) to the intelligible ground of the heart (the ground of all maxims of the will). . ., i.e., for God, this amounts to his actually being a good man (pleasing to Him); and, thus viewed, this change must be regarded as a revolution. *But in the judgement of men, who can appraise themselves and the strength of their maxims only by the ascendancy which they win over their sensuous nature in time, this change must be regarded as nothing but an ever-during (fortdauerndes) struggle toward the better, hence as a gradual reformation of the propensity to evil, the perverted cast of mind.*[40] (my emphasis).

Hence, within the context of the intelligible world – that is, from the perspective of a perfectly rational and divine being – the moral revolution and the new man are distinct, indeed, necessary possibilities. But from the human context, wherein we are inextricably bound to the very source of corruption, the most one can reasonably expect is gradual progress towards an unattainable good. In other words, this progress, or 'reform', since it is bound within the realm of sensibility, must always remain compromised by evil.

However, if the disjunction between good and evil is a manifestation of the dualism between the noumenal and the phenomenal realms, how is it that Kant can even speak of a *relative* moral progress within the latter? The presence of goodness, no matter how limited or fleeting, within the domain of sensuous nature, implies a causality through freedom operative within such nature. And we are, by now, all too familiar with the difficulties involved in any Kantian attempt to sustain this possibility. While it does not seem that Kant is ever able to put this problem to rest, we must acknowledge that he does eventually alter its terms in the manner suggested earlier in this chapter; namely, by characterising the influence of the moral law over sensibility in the image of final, rather than efficient, causality.

THE IDEA OF MORALITY AS A FINAL CAUSE

Not until he is well into the *Critique of Judgement* does Kant consider the contrast between efficient and final concepts of causality. Now, after describing efficient causality as the stand-ard governing a sequence of related events in nature, he notes that 'we are also able to think a causal connection according to a rational concept, that of ends, which, if regarded as a series, would involve regressive as well as progressive dependency. . . A causal nexus of this kind is termed that of final causes'.[41] And, consistent with his contention that the only transcendental ideas of which we can speak with assurance are those inferred from our consciousness of the moral law, Kant goes on to claim that the only being to which we can ascribe final causality is Man, 'but man regarded as noumenon'.[42]

Thus, while efficient causality is a universal principle of nature, the application of which is as extensive as nature itself, final causality is a feature of only one entity – that entity we have found most clearly defined in Kant's concept of the Person – and is, therefore, only efficacious within the context of morality. 'A final end is simply a conception of practical Reason and cannot be inferred from any data of experience for the purpose of forming a theoretical estimate of nature, nor can it be applied to the cognition of nature. The only possible use of this conception is for practical Reason according to moral laws. . .'[43]

With these claims Kant is clearly pointing towards a conception of a moral being as a regulative principle (or, to use his expression, an 'archetype') against which an individual might measure the progress of his or her life's passage. In so doing, Kant is finally providing an illustration of how Reason may become a deter-mining factor within the phenomenal realm, without interfering with or abrogating the constitutive laws of nature. No matter how thoroughly subject we may be to the conditions of experience, we may still judge our behaviour in relation to the image of 'the ought', and do so without for a moment denying the finite and limited character of our existence. And since, for Kant, this image is a condition of our own Reason, the attempt to approximate in practice what we are capable of representing in our moral cognitions does not imply our self-estrangement (that is to say, we are not, thereby, given over to the service of some being or principle foreign to our own nature) but rather, is the highest form of self-expression and a testimony to our capacity for self-determination.

But, if the Kantian ethic is, in the last analysis, free of such alienation, it leaves us with a hauntingly tragic image of the moral life. Both the intellectual and the practical attempt to redeem the mundane but pervasive reality of the here and now, are, from the very outset, destined to fail. '. . .we feel ourselves urged by the moral law to strive after a universal highest end, while we yet feel ourselves, and all nature too, incapable of its attainment'.[44] Thus, while Kant's eventual consideration of final causality helps to mitigate the most extreme implications of the dualism between noumena and phenomena, he is unable to overcome the implications of his earliest characterisations of sentient nature as the antithesis of morality.

In the Kantian scheme of moral things, the religious spirit ultimately prevails over the philosophic. *Knowledge* of the good is supplanted by *belief* in the good. Kant's exquisite attempt, in the first *Critique*, to limit the claims of theoretical understanding eventually exacts its toll upon the equally exquisite effort to construct a pure moral philosophy.

After surveying the broad sweep and evolution of his ethical writings, it requires little by way of further exegesis on our part to see that they present an elaborate variation on a familiar theme. The theme is that of Man as a fallen creature, subject to the temptations of the flesh and unable, through the exercise of his own resources, whether these be those of reason or of the will, to establish a secure foundation for his or her moral capacities: unable, even, to exercise clear ethical judgements over the deeds of either the self or the other. These are within the province of God alone. Reason might disclose the image of moral fulfillment and the possibility, indeed, the necessity of the virtuous life, understood as that which is in accord with the moral law and the autonomous will. But, insofar as Man is a subject with material needs which issue from his sentient nature and can only be answered in nature's world, he is a creature of nature and not of Reason. The tragic conclusion stands exposed in this profound irony: Man, who has his essence and his freedom in the idea of an autonomous self-determination, is unable to determine the issue of his moral redemption.

SUMMARY

Nothing could better exemplify the formal character of Kant's ethics than the bittersweet character of his conclusions. The very conditions which lead him to posit the necessity of a moral revolution and a state of morality as the final end – the profound and irremediable immorality of the lived world – force him to conclude that the revolution, as a secular event, is impossible and the end beyond reach. Freedom and personality are but two of the concepts that would have to be concretised if men and women were to fulfil the promise of their morality. Yet, they were concepts whose reality Kant could demonstrate only through a series of transcendental deductions that systematically expunged the imperatives of the world within which we live and act. Any attempt to restore these considerations, and thereby infuse the concepts of morality (that is, 'freedom', 'the pure will', 'personality', and the 'intelligible world') with substantive meaning would result in the overturning, not only of Kant's ethics, but of the entire Kantian edifice, insofar as it stands astride the twin pillars of phenomenal and noumenal reality.

We shall see that Scheler's Kant-critique moves far in the direction of such an overturning and, as such, represents nothing less than a reversal of Kant's Copernican Revolution. But we shall also find that the insights harboured within Kant's philosophical anthropology are not easily disregarded and that, although Scheler strongly contested the formal nature of Kant's conclusions, he was unable completely to transcend the premises and themes upon which they rested.

3

Scheler, Phenomenology and the Two Orders of Reason

SCHELER AND KANT

A cursory survey of the opening chapters in Scheler's *Der Formalismus in der Ethik und die materiale Wertethik* might leave the impression that Scheler did not take Kant too seriously. As we saw in the introduction to this study, Scheler's references to Kant's first and second *Critiques* are often undocumented and occasionally cited out of context. But to proceed with such an impression would yield an extremely erroneous interpretation of the relationship between Scheler's phenomenological ethics and the contributions made to the study of ethics by Kant's transcendental philosophy. The simple truth behind Scheler's apparently cavalier approach to Kant is that the former's work habits were incompatible with the scholarship required to produce long, well documented treatises. 'Restless in the quiet of a library or study, he preferred the bustle of chattering people and the clink of glasses, even for his most serious writing. Because he did much of his "research" in restaurants and cafés, his notes scribbled on the back of a menu or letter, he found it difficult to trace the sources of many of his ideas'.[1] We are cautioned, then, not to confuse the substance of Scheler's Kant-critique with the manner of its presentation: the best of philosophy is often nurtured in unorthodox settings.

Moreover, there are several clear indications that Scheler approached Kant's work in earnest, indeed with respect. When, in 1916, Scheler presented the first Preface to the *Formalismus*, he hastened to acknowledge that the work he was about to challenge severely was 'the most consummate ethic which we today possess'. (FORM 9) In fact, it was precisely because he

46

considered the Kantian ethic the paradigm expression of ethical formalism that Scheler chose to address his critique explicitly to Kant rather than to formalism in general. He was convinced that Kant's work was nothing less than 'a colossus of steel and bronze', which could withstand or assimilate any superficial objections. All attempts to refute Kant's doctrine by denouncing its most obvious shortcomings had, in Scheler's judgement, either failed completely or achieved only a slight modification of the original position they set out to refute. Accordingly, only a critique addressed to the very roots of Kant's thought – that is, to his presuppositions and premises – could ever succeed in moving beyond Kant's conclusions.

Why then, if he held Kant's work in such high esteem, did Scheler feel such a critique was necessary? Again, most simply, because of his conviction that unless the means were developed to surpass the Kantian ethic we would be denied 'any view into the fullness of the moral world and any conviction about our ability to achieve binding relationships with that world'. (FORM 30) In a word, Scheler was interested in establishing a rigorous philosophical foundation for an ethics of flesh and blood, not one of bronze and steel.

Thus, the relationship between Scheler's material ethics and the ethical formalism which pervades Kant's ethics is a rich example of continuity and discontinuity in the history of philosophy. From the outset Scheler saw his work as an extension, rather than a subversion of Kant's. His purpose is to lay the foundation for a philosophical ethic that might address itself to the material content of our moral experience with the same precision and certainty Kant seeks to achieve in his explication of the formal elements of that experience. Although Scheler does not employ the term, his relationship with Kant could be described – in a metaphorical, if not philosophic, sense – as dialectical. At many points his arguments develop along lines that are in direct opposition to those of Kant. But where this opposition tends towards the establishment of positions that seem to contradict basic tenets of the formal ethics, this is not the mode of contradiction we encounter in analytic philosophy. We are not, for example, asked to choose between 'A' and 'not-A' – between Kant and Scheler – but to see Kant's rational humanism as 'a moment in the history of spirit', and, presumably, a moment that will be contained, rather than cancelled, by Scheler's ethic of material values (*materiale Wertehik*). (FORM 20) At other points Scheler is in explicit agreement with Kant and it is these which deserve our initial attention.

The main Kantian doctrine that is preserved, more or less intact, within Scheler's ethics is the former's rejection of any ethics grounded in the anticipated realisation of some finite good or end. (Scheler characterises such ethics as *die Güterethik* and *die Zweckethik*.) With respect to the former he writes,

> . . .as Kant says, whenever we make the goodness or evil of a person, an act of will, an activity, and the like, dependent upon their relation to some established world of prevailing goods we also make the goodness or evil of the will dependent upon the particular and contingent being of this world of goods (*Güterwelt*). . . With the alteration of this world of goods the sense and meaning of good and evil will also change. . . Any world of goods can be partially subverted by the power of nature or history. If our will were morally dependent upon this world then it too would be subverted.

Thus, to make the will dependent upon the contingency that characterises the realm of things and events is, 'as Kant rightly saw, obvious nonsense'. (FORM 32) The same considerations apply to any attempts to define the goodness or evil of the will in terms of some end, 'be it an end for the world, for humanity, an end or goal of mankind's aspirations, or a so-called final end (*Endzweck*'. Any ethic which proceeds in this manner reduces the value of good and evil to the status of a mere technique for the achieving of whatever end is preferred or chosen. But, 'ends are only legitimate if the will which assigns them their value is a good will'. (FORM 33)

Two comments need to be made upon these claims and the implicit interpretation of Kant from which they spring. First, Scheler is not denying the *reality* of the values that comprise a world of goods, for example, the constellation of values that surround such notions as private property or the nation-state.[2] Rather, he is highlighting their relative and historical character – 'goods' such as private property and the state are features of particular forms of social organisation – and objecting to any ethic that would promote them as an absolute standard for morality. Thus we have, at the very outset of the *Formalismus*, a clear anticipation of how strenuously Scheler will strive to establish an absolute (non-contingent and *a priori* foundation for his ethics).

Second, insofar as the above remarks are more in keeping with the spirit than the letter of Kant's doctrine, they yield a typical illustration of the manner in which Scheler reads Kant. With respect to the question of an ethic of ends, there can be little doubt that Kant rejects any morality that makes the goodness of the will contingent upon historical considerations. But, Kant's own stance is, as we have seen, much more ambiguous than Scheler's overly inclusive generalisations would indicate. Kant's quarrel is with any ethic that seeks to determine the morality of the will in some end external or foreign to the will, rather than with the notion of a final end as such. Within the compass of the will and its determinations he does not preclude the notion of a final end, but, on the contrary, explicitly contends that the idea of the moral law is, for the will and practical Reason, final.

Scheler's comments on the subject of an ethic of goods also represent a rather imprecise reading of Kant. Again, while his conclusions are in harmony with those of Kant, the latter's arguments are grounded in considerations germaine to the structure of the first *Critique*, rather than in preoccupations that emerge from a study of psychology or history. We will recall that the crucial matter, for Kant, is that no ethics that makes the satisfaction of phenomenal or physical needs and desires its primary concern can ever achieve the formulation of *a priori* principles. This last point is particularly important because as we move further into Scheler's Kant-critique we shall see that the question of the *a priori*, that is, the nature and compass of what cognition and sensibility can be legitimately said to bring to experience, is at the heart of Scheler's disagreement with Kant.

We have noted that Scheler was chiefly concerned with the premises of Kant's philosophy and that, arguably, this fact contributed to his lack of attention to the details of Kant's elaborate system of critiques. But, there is a more profound matter at issue here; namely, the circumstance of Scheler's place within a philosophical movement (namely, phenomenology) that was engaged in a radical questioning of the premises which had sustained modern, post-Cartesian philosophy and science. If Scheler felt capable of criticising the Kantian account of experience this was, in large measure, because his understanding of what phenomenology entailed provided him with the method and direction for such a critique. Indeed, we can say that the most fundamental difference between Scheler and Kant is the difference between the respective *Weltanschauungen* of phenomenology and eighteenth-century rationalism. But, an appreciable assessment of this difference requires some preliminary observations on Scheler's more immediate objections to the Kantian ethic.

SCHELER'S THEORY OF VALUES

Once he establishes those areas in which he concurs with Kant, Scheler begins that critical commentary which is one of the sustaining chords of the *Formalismus*. His first claim is that Kant, having correctly shown that neither the goods nor ends to which the will is directed provide sufficient grounds for ethics, goes one step further to deny any decisive role to all values of a material nature. As evidence Scheler cites the first Theorem of the *Critique of Practical Reason*. 'All practical principles which presuppose an object (matter) of the faculty of desire as the determining ground of the will are empirical and can furnish no practical laws'. Behind this Theorem, Scheler asserts, stands one of the tacit presuppositions of Kant, namely, that the axiological features of the goods and ends we desire are ontologically distinct from the goods or ends themselves, and that it is therefore possible to speak of such values as 'justice', 'injustice', 'good', and 'evil', in terms of the *formal* relationships which prevail between the will and its ends, without dealing with specific instantiations of willing and desiring. Scheler ascribes to Kant the further assumption that prior to, and independent of, the moment when the will assigned itself a particular goal there was no moment when the will was influenced by values. (FORM 34) The gist of this charge is that Kant believes he can adequately discuss the phenomena of willing and desiring in purely formal terms without taking under consideration the material content of our desires and preferences, that is, the *values* towards which the will is directed or strives; in Scheler's lexicon, the objects of our conation or endeavour (*Streben*). Scheler is convinced that herein lies the key to Kant's confusion *vis-à-vis* the material of moral experience and that, in fact, the will *and* its objects constitute a unity that cannot be sundered without doing violence to such experience.

In support of these claims, Scheler first considers the relationship between goods and values (*Güter und Werte*) in an attempt to show that since there is a fundamental difference between them, Kant's rejection of any decisive ethical function for goods need not entail a rejection of a similar role for material values. Undoubtedly, he argues, such values as 'the agreeable', 'the charming', 'the noble', and 'the elegant', first appear to us in proximity with people and things. But, in Scheler's account, this does not mean that they are inseparable properties of people and things, any more than colours are inseparable from the states and objects with which they appear. 'Just as we can conceive of red as an extensive quality in a pure colour spectrum, so we can understand values . . . as originally accessible to us as pure and extensive qualities even though they pertain to men and things'. (FORM 35) Citing another example, Scheler points out that aesthetic values are not reducible to the common properties of things. If we search for the beauty, the charm, or the attractiveness of a vase, a flower, or a horse, by considering their common properties we come up empty handed. In order to make such aesthetic judgements we must already have been given these values as affecting the things we are judging. In other words, we bring our sensibility or feeling for beauty to the perception of the beautiful flower. The same consideration holds true of ethical experience. We do not, Scheler contends, become aware of the goodness or evil, the courage or cowardice, of individuals and deeds through the constant characterisation of particular men, women, and deeds as good or evil, courageous or cowardly. On the contrary, we can grasp the essence of these values in the condition of a single individual or a single deed. Thus it is erroneous to look for the good and the evil in terms of common or shared properties, rather than recognise that a value can only be given intuitively or be grounded in the antecedent perception of a value which is so given. 'Just as it is senseless to ask about the common property of all red and blue things, since the only possible answer could be that some are blue and others are red, so it is senseless to ask about the common properties of good and evil actions.' (FORM 37) And, just as the colour blue does not change when I paint a blue ball red, so too, 'the value of friendship is not impugned if my friend proves treacherous and betrays me'. (FORM 41)

I find these observations persuasive evidence for Scheler's contention that values are neither reducible to, not interchangeable with, the specific objects or states through which they become empirically apparent to us, that is, with goods. And, once the plausibility of Scheler's distinction between values and goods is admitted, it would seem that, indeed, he does establish an arguable case for his assertion that Kant's rejection of goods need not necessarily entail a rejection of material values.

However, on this point Scheler's Kant-critique involves much more than the claim that Kant's attempt to discuss the will and its activities without reference to material values was *unnecessary*: in Scheler's view Kant was seeking a level of abstraction it is *impossible* to attain. Access to the transcendental ideals and principles is impossible because our most primordial relationship with the world is infused and coloured by the perception of values (*Wertnehmung*) and this perception – or 'value-ception' – can never be excluded from any judgements that are made subsequent to it. To illustrate his point, Scheler cites those fairly common instances in which our first acquaintance with a woman, man, or object is charged with the perception of some value. We may find a man repulsive or agreeable, and perceive a work of art to be beautiful or ugly, before we have time to analyse those properties and features that have provoked our reaction. Indeed, if and when we undertake such an analysis, it will be guided and influenced by our initial *Wertnehmung*. And, this is not the isolated and occasional phenomenon these examples might suggest. The priority of *Wertnehmung* is, on the contrary, universal. In what his most sensitive and sympathetic English language commentator has described 'the fundamental message' of Scheler's ethics,[3] Scheler writes,

... every mode of intellectual-comprehension-of-whatness (*Soseinserfassung*) of an object *presupposes* an *emotional* experience of *value* which bears upon the object. This proposition is valid for the simplist perception as well as for remembering, expecting, and finally, for all modes of thinking: it is valid for the intuition of primordial phenomena (*Urphänomene*) (that is, the basic structure of things exclusive of all sensation and determinate existence) and for immediate conceptualisation (*unmittelbare Ideendenken*), which both lead to *a priori* knowledge. It is valid for all cognition of fortuitous facts which are founded on observation, induction, and immediate thought; value-ception (*Wertnehmung*) always precedes perception. The first words of a child contain wish and the expression-of-feeling (*Gefühlsausdruck*). However, psychic expression is also that which is perceived first. The child comprehends that sugar is 'agreeable' before he comprehends that sugar is 'sweet'.[4]

Clearly, this remarkable statement has implications that go far beyond Scheler's critique of Kant, implications we will consider in subsequent chapters. For the moment, however, we can confine ourselves to the observation that its consequences for the foundational principles of Kant's formalism are telling. If, for example, Scheler is correct in stating that *Wertnehmung* is a fundamental and integral feature of all conceptualisation, the very possibility of a categorical imperative is in jeopardy, Kant's contention that it is possible to determine the will in a purely formal manner is insupportable, and the idea of a pure 'ought' is chimerical. For, granting Scheler's claim, the very suggestion of an 'ought' presupposes the recognition of some value that should be instantiated, that is some *material* object of the will. '. . . wherever an ought (*einem Sollen*) is spoken of, the comprehension of a value must already have taken place.' (FORM 193) To be sure, the categorical imperative or moral law can be *a* factor in the determinations of the will. But,

an ideal ought such as 'one should be good' becomes a demand because it is simultaneously experienced in reference to some content which may be realised through an effort (of the will). Only on these grounds is it possible to ask the questions 'what should I do, what should I be'? If the ought were solely and originally a demand or an experienced initiative. . . these questions would never be raised and the problem of the will's obligation to achieve some state of being would never exist. (FORM 218)

The crux of this objection is that Kant assumed the question of 'what should I do?' can be answered by considering only *how* we act, that is, to the form of the will's determination. However, as the original question suggests, the *what* of the will's activity – the specific value to be affirmed or denied – is a crucial factor in the will's determinations, preferences and choices. Moreover, Scheler is arguing that, even that instance in which Kant believes the will is determined by form alone, namely, when the will acts in accord with the moral law, must be seen as an instance of material determination. 'Even where the idea of the law is determining the will, that law is still *material* for the will.' And, rather than being the only manner in which a pure will can consummate itself (*sich vollzöge*) the realisation of the moral law is simply 'one of the possible materials of the will'. (FORM 81)

From the Kantian point of view, Scheler's attempt to assign the moral law a place alongside other possible objects of the will would seriously challenge the special authority of the moral law, since it clearly denies such a law its privileged standing in ethics. However, a different picture emerges if we consider this development in light of Scheler's concern to found an ethics which will be able to speak to the fullness of our moral experience. We have already seen that Scheler would repudiate any moral philosophy that has its origins in some special world of goods, that is, objects which are valued insofar as they reflect the interests or desires of a particular group, institution, culture or individual. But once he establishes the distinction between values and goods, he is able to speak of values as autonomous and essential objects of the will, rather than as properties relative and subordinate to the articles, events, people and states with which they appear. In effect, this development represents a distancing of values from their empirical 'bearers', (*Trägers*) and, as such, an *elevation* of values to the standing Kant had reserved for the moral law alone.

Here we have a clear instance of what Scheler has in mind when he characterises his work as an 'extension' of Kant's. By claiming for values an essential place within the realm of the will's moral activity, Scheler does not depreciate the worth of the moral law any more than the arrival of a new child in the family diminishes the worth of its previous and present members. On the contrary, the moral realm – like the domain of the family – is considerably enriched.

However, we are still at that stage in the discussion where we have to say that the moral realm 'would' be enriched, 'if' Scheler's account of values as the essential objects of the will 'were' correct. These qualifications will remain until and unless Scheler answers the demand, which he shares with Kant, for an ethic grounded in *a priori* knowledge. The distinction between values and goods moves Scheler a step closer to that goal, since it indicates that values need not share in the relativism which characterises any *Güterethik*. But this is certainly not enough to accomplish Scheler's intent. It is quite possible to agree with the distinction he draws between values and goods, while still maintaining that since the recognition of values is contingent upon experience any knowledge this recognition might yield must be *a posteriori*. Indeed, by insisting on the elemental value-character of all experience, Scheler would seem to preclude the very possibility of *a priori* knowledge and, consequently, of a universally binding ethic. If all cognition and perception is charged with an antecedent perception of value, how can we ever aspire to knowledge that is independent of all experience?

This last question can only be answered in Scheler's favour if he can show that any knowledge which might originate in *Wertnehmung* is not necessarily *a posteriori*, if that is, he can demonstrate the possibility of a material *a priori*. In his own terms, Scheler must answer the question: 'is there a *material ethic* which is at the same time *a priori*, in the sense that its propositions are evident and require neither observation nor induction for their affirmation or refutation?' (FORM 67)

Once again, Scheler's arguments are framed within the context of the Kant-critique. Specifically, he seeks to show that Kant commits a fundamental error by identifying the *a priori* with the formal where, in truth, 'the opposition between *a priori* and *a posteriori* does not have the least to do with that between the *formal* and the *material*. (FORM 72) However, it is no longer sufficient for an understanding of Scheler's claims to note that he is still working out his dispute with Kant. The case for material *a priori* knowledge is a contribution of Scheler's phenomenology, and thus, any adequate understanding of his argument must be prefaced by and embrace some consideration for his relationship to the phenomenological philosophy, as well as the manner in which he appropriated its method and insights in the pursuit of his own philosophical purposes.

SCHELER AND PHENOMENOLOGY

The 'mission' of phenomenology is heralded in Edmund Husserl's challenge for philosophy to 'return to the things themselves'. This appeal was prompted by the conviction that if philosophers would provisionally suspend all preconceptions and judgements pertaining to spatio-temporal existence (*Dasein*) – whether they were judgements about the physical existence of objects, relationships between these objects, or the nature of the psyche – and give their thoughts over to a study of that which is revealed in the 'flow of phenomena' which remains, philosophy could once more become engaged in the study of essential states of being.

The first step in the phenomenological method must, then, entail a willful abstention or a 'bracketing' from consideration of the whole world; 'including ourselves and our thinking'.[5] If we are not seriously to misunderstand Husserl on this point, we must note that with this bracketing or suspension – this *epoche* – he is not seeking to deny the existence of the empirical world. He simply denies, for the moment, the authority of the 'naturalistic thesis', that is, he denies himself recourse to any propositions or theories that are grounded in the postulation of a 'natural world'.[6] With the performance of the *epoche* the philosopher is, Husserl claims, in the presence of pure experiences (*Erlebnisse*) or phenomena. And, with a careful and methodical description of these phenomena the philosopher can legitimately aspire to a knowledge of their essential natures.

One way of catching Husserl's intent is to watch him at work with the phenomenological method. In his analysis of consciousness, for example, he beings by abstaining from any judgements with respect to either the subject of consciousness (the Ego) or its object (the natural world). With these features bracketed he is free to concentrate all his attention (in an act described as 'eidetic intuition') on the intrinsic features of consciousness itself.[7] Reflecting upon what is given in this intuition he discovers, in Paul Ricoeur's phrase, consciousness 'as a bursting out beyond itself'.[8] He discovers, in other words, the essence of consciousness in its intentionality: consciousness is always conscious-ness of some-thing. And, since he is still reflecting within the context of the *epoche*, every objective correlate of consciousness has the same ontic status as every other. Empirical existence, for example, does not become the standard against which Husserl measures illusory existence. On the contrary, it makes no difference here whether the thing (*Sache*) intended by consciousness is fictitious (Hamlet), illusory (a desert mirage), or a 'real' entity in space and time (this typewriter). All are equally legitimate subjects for phenomenological inquiry and all, when submitted to eidetic intuition, are capable of being known as they truly are.

These admittedly brief and oversimplified observations only serve to carry us across the threshold of Husserlian phenomenology. For its founder, phenomenology remained a constant problematic, an enterprise to be continually reworked, amended and questioned. For Scheler, on the other hand, the situation was quite different. As Moritz Geiger puts it so well,

What attracted him to phenomenology was not the analysis and separation of the phenomena carried out in strictest discipline . . . . Scheler, who rushed ahead with his characteristic brilliance, was not made for checking and counter-checking. For him something different was essential in phenomenology; he had discovered in it a method of intuition. . . Its primary objective was to grasp what is given. It allowed one, and even made it a duty, to intuit plainly and simply, prior to constructive systematising and to genetic considerations. . . no one possessed the capacity for such intuition (*Schau*) to a higher degree than Scheler but . . . no one was equally exposed to the danger inherent in phenomenological intuition, as in every intuition, that what *seems* to be intuited and what has been seized without proper examination is taken for something really intuited.[9]

We have already seen, in our discussion of Scheler's account of values, evidence of the capacity for intuition which Geiger describes here. And we shall have further occasion to observe Scheler making unwarranted claims for phenomenological intuition. For the moment, however, we can note that phenomenology was never the self-contained enterprise for Scheler that it was for Husserl. Rather, it was the 'great tool which could bring about a decisive reform of our *Weltanschauung*'.[10]

THE MATERIAL *A PRIORI*

Returning now to the mainstream of our discussion, it is clear that phenomenology represents a departure from Kant's transcendental idealism in at least two significant respects. First, knowledge of the phenomenal realm is no longer limited to appearances within space and time, appearances of the unknowable things-in-themselves. Rather, the phenomenal realm here assumes the status of a medium which, if faithfully and adequately described, will yield knowledge of the thing-in-itself. The *epoche* removes, to employ the Kantian term, the spatio-temporal manifold and with it the whole field of appearances, leaving us, as it were, in the company of essences. Phenomenology thus seeks to undermine the Kantian dichotomy between phenomena and noumena. Second, the range of that which comprises legitimately known experience is considerably enlarged. Experience is no longer limited to empirical knowledge of appearances, while veridical thought is no longer restricted to that which is necessarily implied in such experience. Thus, in its relation to the critical philosophy of Kant, phenomenology offers a liberated and expansive vista of cognition. We can readily appreciate the sense of excitement with which Scheler read the early work of Husserl. And, more specifically, we are now able to see how phenomenology enforced and aided Scheler's attempt to provide a philosophical foundation for the possibility of material *a priori* knowledge.

Within the realm of the *a priori* Scheler includes 'all those ideal units of meaning (*Bedeutungseinheiten*) and propositions which become self-evident within, and by means of, an *immediate intuition*, without positing anything about the thinking subjects and their natural constitution and without positing anything about the objects to which they would be applicable'. (FORM 67)[11] Lest there be any doubt that Scheler is working here within the rubric of phenomenology, he goes on to make the linkage between his conception of the *a priori* and the phenomena explicit. 'We call the content of such an intuition a "phenomenon", thus, the "phenomenon" has nothing to do with the "appearance" of an existent or with the "apparent". Such a manner of intuition is "essential intuition" (*Wesensschau*), or, as we will say, *"phenomenological intuition"* or *"phenomenological experience"*.' (FORM 68) We have already observed that this conception of the phenomenon would render Kant's dualism of the phenomenal and the noumenal meaningless. But, Scheler goes one step further to claim that the essence given in phenomenological experience is, 'as such, neither universal nor particular. Only the relationship to the object, in which an essent (*Wesenheit*) makes its appearance (*Erscheinung*), reveals its significance as universal or particular'. (FORM 68) 'An essent becomes *universal* if it appears in identical form with a plurality of different objects (*Gegenstände*), all of which "have" or "bear" the same essence. But it can also constitute the essence of an individual without ceasing to be an essent.' (FORM 68)

Earlier we saw Scheler claim that it is possible to grasp the essence of a value in the condition or activity of a single individual. At that point in his reflections the claim was supported solely by an appeal to common sense. Now, by conjoining his analysis of the material *a priori* with the phenomenological analysis of experience, Scheler is able to achieve, at the very least, the semblance of an epistemological foundation.

Phenomenological experience is for Scheler, then, an experience of *a priori* states and structures – 'essents and relationships between them' – which may become manifest in either a particular or a universal context. (FORM 68) The distance between this formulation and Kant's is indicated by the fact that universality, which was one of the two conditions Kant demanded of all *a priori* conditions and knowledge, is no longer considered a vital factor. (FORM 94) Yet, we should not infer from this that Scheler denies universality any place or role in *a priori* knowledge. He does not, for example, challenge the fact that the propositions of formal logic, that is, the law of contradiction, must apply in each and every case. What he does challenge is any assertion that such propositions are grounded in the activity of the understanding, and that their truth is a function of the laws of thought.

> The *a priori* is neither bound to the propositions or the acts of judgement of which propositions speak, something like a *form* of these propositions and acts (that is, the forms of judgement out of which Kant developed his categories as law-giving functions of thought); but it belongs completely to the things which are given (*zum Gegegenen*), to the realm of the factual (*Tatsachensphäre*). A proposition is only *a priori* true insofar as it has been realised in fact. (FORM 68–69)

Thus, if a proposition is *a priori* true it is true because it is a reflection of the actual state of affairs; not because it conforms to the rules of thought or logic. In the final analysis the validity of all propositions, indeed all knowledge worthy of being deemed such, is grounded in phenomenological experience, that is, in the intuition of essences and relationships between them (*Wesenszusammenhänge*).

Scheler does not give us specific illustrations of his argument, but this is surely not because they are difficult to find. For example, his intent is clarified by the observation that I know the oxymoronic quality of a term such as 'the square-circle', not because I have tried unsuccessfully to juxtapose circles on to squares or vice versa, and not because I have examined their respective definitions and found them mutually exclusive; but because I find it impossible to maintain, in the same intuition, the image of a square and the image of a circle. In this account, 'A is B and A is not B', is a false proposition only by virtue of a phenomenological insight into the *fact* that the being and non-being of some thing (given in intuition) are incompatible'. (FORM 72)

It is in the same spirit that we are to understand the following propositions of Scheler's *materiale Wertethik*. Each of them rests upon a phenomenological intuition of a necessary relationship between values, rather than upon observation or induction.

I. 1. The existence of a positive value is itself a positive value.
   2. The non-existence of a positive value is itself a negative value.
   3. The existence of a negative value is itself a negative value.
   4. The non-existence of a negative value is itself a positive value.
II. 1. Good is that value in the sphere of the will which adheres (*haftet*) to the realisation of a positive value.
    2. Evil is that value in the sphere of the will which adheres to the realisation of a negative value.
    3. Good is that value in the sphere of the will which adheres to the realisation of a higher (or highest) value.
    4. Evil is that value, which in the sphere of the will, adheres to the realisation of a lower (or lowest) value. (FORM 48)

It is not surprising that Scheler's constant appeal to intuition as the ultimate test of *a priori* truth has often provoked his readers to ascribe to his thought an unwarranted degree of emotivism that often tends towards sheer irrationalism.[12] In his defence it should be noted that even Kant allows for a type of knowledge whereby thought is in the immediate presence of its objects. However, where Kant limited such knowledge to space and time, as the 'two pure forms of sensible intuition' (A 22), Scheler's intention is to achieve a perspective wherein philosophy might approach all of its subject matter at this pre-conceptual and elemental level. It is not necessary to level charges of irrationalism against Scheler to make the point that this ambition is, as Geiger remarks, exceedingly difficult to carry out and comprehend. As we shall see, it harbours at least one potential flaw which becomes more and more prominent as Scheler's ethics unfold.

THE MATERIALIST REDUCTION

In the Introduction to this study I suggested that Scheler's understanding of the term 'material' in the concept of a *materiale Wertethik* could best be clarified after we had observed its function in *Der Formalismus*. We are now able to see that his use of the term is indeed contextual and that, moreover, the setting in and from which it derives its significance is marked by two dominant themes. First, it is clear that Scheler conceives of the 'material' in Kantian terms, which is to say, as that which stands in opposition to the purely formal elements of experience and thought. The title of *Der Formalismus* and practically every turn in the explication of the material *a priori* contain an explicit reference to the Kantian distinction between the formal and material realms. However, with the introduction of the phenomenological analysis of experience (the second contextual theme) the distinction Kant labours so persistently first to establish and then to sustain, begins to break down and a radically modified image of the 'material' emerges.

Within the Kantian frame of reference the material of experience comprises the sensations present in the spatio-temporal manifold, or that which is given in *empirical* intuition. And, we will recall that experience so defined constitutes the limit beyond which thought cannot stray without encountering contradictions it is unable definitively to resolve. But, with phenomenology's enlarged vista of cognitive experience there is a corresponding expansive notion of what constitutes the material of experience. The data of *consciousness* and not simply the data of sensation are now taken as legitimate objects for study and analysis: the mode of comprehension is now described as *essential*, rather than *empirical*, intuition.

One result of this development is that the distinction between the formal and the material, like that between the phenomenal and the noumenal, begins to collapse. Just as Husserl's definition of the phenomenon include the Kantian noumenon (the thing-in-itself), so too Scheler's conception of the material *a priori* includes those propositions and activities to which Kant assigned only a purely formal standing. Thus, we find Scheler claiming that the moral law, which for Kant is expressed *formally* as the categorical imperative, is in fact, *material* for the will. This is a claim wholly consistent with Scheler's ambition to demonstrate the possibility of material *a priori* knowledge, particularly since such an effort includes the contention that formal propositions are expressions of relationships between essents that are themselves grounded in the essential or 'material' intuition of some state of affairs. And yet, once Scheler has made the identification between the content of essential intuition and the substance of material *a priori* knowledge, it is difficult to see how he can preserve any distinction between the form and matter of experience. The problem becomes especially acute when we recall that the demonstration of the material *a priori* is carried out within the phenomenological *epoche*, where all the data which appear before consciousness enjoy the same ontic status. If Scheler is to remain faithful to the phenomenological perspective, it would seem that once he has defined the objects of essential intuition – whether these are the propositions of formal logic or the values disclosed in the analysis of *Wertnehmung* – as 'material', he must admit that this term has now acquired a connotation that tends to dissolve the traditional distinction between form and matter.

To my knowledge, Scheler never explicitly acknowledges this problem, which I have chosen to call the 'materialist reduction'. This may simply be a reflection of the fact that his primary concern is not with the phenomenological attitude as such, but rather with phenomenology as a method to be employed (or appropriated) insofar as it serves his larger interests. To a great extent he employed the method most effectively in the critical portions of his writings (most prominently in the Kant-critique). We shall see that as he begins to knit together the threads of his earlier claims and arguments, while moving on to the more original and distinctive features of his own ethics, he also moves from a phenomenological to a metaphysical and speculative mode of reflection.

THE TWO ORDERS OF REASON

The cumulative effect of Scheler's critique is the undermining of Kant's transcendental idealism. Each of the distinctions Kant seeks to sustain – between noumena and phenomena, the *a priori* and the *a posteriori*, and the formal and the material elements of experience – assigned responsibility for whatever order and coherence we find *in the world* to the activity of a thinking subject. Lest we be misled on this point, we should recall that Kant does not thereby intend to preclude the possibility of our thinking of a supersensible realm of nature. Indeed, Kant insists upon the right of Reason to postulate the *idea* of a purely intelligible being 'that is free from all empirical conditions and itself contains the ground of the possibility of all appearances'. (A 562, B 590) This, and other regulative principles of reason, which differ from the constitutive principles of reason in that they do not determine the knowledge of appearances, may 'be admitted as a transcendental object, but only if we admit that, for the rest, we have no (determinate) knowledge of it'. (A 565, B 593) 'Reason proceeds by one path in its empirical use, and by yet another path in its transcendental use'. (A 563, B 591) In brief, Kant's is a transcendental, not a subjective, idealism.

With Scheler's phenomenological analysis we have seen the gradual disintegration of these distinctions. It is not surprising, then, that Scheler eventually turns his attention to the ultimate Kantian dichotomy, namely that between thought (which provides the categories and activity *for* knowledge) and sensibility (which contains the material to be organised into a coherent body *of* knowledge. This schema, according to Scheler, is a result of Kant's unwarranted acceptance of the Humean claim that what is given in sensibility is a chaos of unstructured and unrelated data. (FORM 85) So long as we accept this view, Scheler argues, we will necessarily have recourse to something like Kant's synthetic function of the understanding to account for the appearance of an ordered and lawful universe: 'Humean nature needs a Kantian understanding to exist'. (FORM 85) On the other hand, if Hume was in error – if that which is immediately given in sensibility exhibits an order of its own, prior to any acts of induction or deduction – then the elaborate rationalism Kant develops becomes superfluous. This alternative is, of course, the one towards which Scheler moves with his demonstration of a material *a priori*, and his claim that even the laws of thought are grounded in essential intuitions.

At issue here are two radically different and opposed accounts of experience. In the Kantian view, experience is a synthetic construction designed and carried out by thought. Hence, whoever would understand the order we find in the world must begin by describing the nature of thought. For Scheler, this is an approach that conceals more than it reveals. In the end such an effort must become entrapped in a massive 'symbolism' that is, at best, a reflection of reality. The truth is far better served by attending closely and faithfully to what is given *to* consciousness, rather than by dwelling upon the internal processes of the rational consciousness themselves. For Kant the idea of a pre-conceptual experience is profoundly mystifying; for Scheler it is reality itself.

Yet (and, with all that has led him to this point, somewhat surprisingly) Scheler does not deny the existence of a rational order. Put most simply, his claim is that such is not the only order, that there is, in Pascal's phrase, an order or logic of the heart: 'the emotions of the spirit; feeling, preference, love, hate, and *willing* have original *a priori* contents which borrow nothing from thought'. (FORM 82) And Scheler is careful to point out that when Pascal cited the 'reasons of the heart', he meant *reasons*.

> ... an eternal and absolute lawful order (*Gesetzmässigkeit*) of feeling, love, and hate that is as absolute as that of pure logic but that is in no way reducible to the lawful order of the intellect... there is a mode of experience whose objects are completely barred from the intellect and to which the intellect is as blind as the ear and hearing are to colours. And this is a mode of experience which conveys to us genuine objects and an eternal order between them, to wit, values and a hierarchy between them. (FORM 260, 261)

SUMMARY

At the heart of these passages, which I read as the culmination of Scheler's Kant-critique – although, as we shall see, the preoccupation with Kant's ethics continue to serve as a counterpoint to the elaboration of Scheler's own position – there is a serious ambiguity. Throughout this presentation we have watched Scheler move towards what I earlier characterised as a reversal of Kant's Copernican Revolution. We need only recall that the character of the *a priori* has been reformulated in a way that provides thought with knowledge of the things-in-themselves. Further, the articulation of the material *a priori* holds out the promise that, with Scheler, philosophy might free itself from the Kantian legacy of an anthropology that portrays Man as a being twice tormented, divided within between the dictates of his noumenal and phenomenal natures, while estranged from the ultimate meaning of that which surrounds him. If the phenomenological method is able to disclose the essential structures and meanings upon which the Kantian edifice is constructed, then transcendental experience becomes nothing more than an impoverished and derivative substitute for phenomenological experience.

But, at the very moment when he seems about to pursue this line of thought and thereby heal the rift between phenomenal and noumenal Man, Scheler reinstates Kant's distinction between a realm of sensibility – now characterised as 'the order of the heart' – and a lawful order of reason. Kant's claim that Reason cannot address itself with any certainty to the content of our feelings is upheld, and phenomenological experience is offered as simply an alternative to transcendental experience.

To be sure, the alternative is richer than its Kantian counterpart. And Scheler's phenomenology of the emotional life will reveal dimensions of sensibility Kant is unable to address. But, as we take up Scheler's exposition of the hierarchy of values and his concept of the Person, we will find his failure to completely overcome Kant's distinction between thought and sensibility, together with the 'materialist reduction', combining to constitute the root problem of his material ethics.

Part II
The Material Ethics
of Value

4
Scheler's Hierarchy of Values

As we traced the major stages of Scheler's Kant-critique we repeatedly observed the extent to which Scheler insists upon the cognitive primacy of what is variously characterised as the perception of value (*Wertnehmung*) or the emotional experience of value (*emotionale Werterlebnis*). We noted his contention that this phenomenon precedes and colours all intellectual judgements (including judgements of value themselves) and, insofar as it finds the content of values an indispensable element in any act of valuation, precludes the possibility of a purely formal ethics. But the fruits of Scheler's attention to the realm of sensibility are far from exhausted in the critical or negative phase of his ethical studies. By attending closely to that which is manifest in our experience of values, he claims for cognition access to the domain of values itself and the capacity to record the *a priori* structures and distinctions therein. There should be little doubt that the results of this ambitious, if not unprecedented, enterprise have made a significant contribution to the vast literature which has accumulated over the centuries, and now comprise a wealth of reflections and insights into the possibilities present in humanity's normative and moral experience. This is the case despite the fact that Scheler, no less than the greatest moral philosophers who preceded him and, hopefully, those who will follow him, does not give us the definitive work he seems to strive for; and despite the fact that, as I will continue to contend, he did not totally succeed in his effort to overcome the Kantian distinction between thought and sensibility, between Man as spirit and Man as creature.

VORZIEHEN AS EVIDENCE FOR A HIERARCHY OF VALUES

Among Scheler's more insightful observations on the character of normative experience is his insistence that such experience is contextual, rather than discrete. In other words, he reminds us that rarely, if ever, is a value given in isolation from other values. Rather, the perception of any value carries with it the implication of other values which are assigned a higher or lower (*höher oder niedriger*) status in relation to it. In support of this observation Scheler notices how the perception of any value is usually accompanied by feelings of preference (*Vorziehen*) or depreciation (*Nachsetzen*).[1] 'That one value is higher than another is comprehended in a particular act of value cognition (*Werterkenntnis*) that is called "preference".' (FORM 105)

Once again it seems worth our while to illustrate Scheler's intention with the examples he is so reluctant to supply. If I express a preference for the fiction of Gabriel García Márquez I do so against the background – or within the experience – of other literature. Whether I explicitly take note of the fact or not, my preference for Márquez assigns his work a higher value than that of others I have enjoyed: the Faulkners, the Conrads, the Fitzgeralds and so on. Similarly, a preference for roses carries an implicit value-judgement upon the beauty of other flowers while the commitment to democracy says a great deal about the worthiness of other political and social orders. All expressions of value preference or rejection, then, call forth and render judgement upon items from the species of things preferred or rejected. Nonetheless, as these examples indicate, our value preferences provide only the suggestion of *some* order or scale of values. They tell us little about which values are or should be recognised as highest.

Scheler himself is well aware that, as often as not, our preferences are nothing more nor less than the expression of subjective tastes and interests. Accordingly, his claim for what we might learn from *Vorziehen* is a limited one. The phenomenon of preference may yield some intimation of the absolute and invariable hierarchy of values he is striving to articulate but, in itself, can only provide evidence for an order of preference (*Vorzugsregeln*) that varies from individual to individual, generation to generation, and culture to culture. Yet, for the moment, Scheler is satisfied with having shown that there are *any* hierarchical relationships given in normative experience. For, once this is established, he is able to resort to the distinction he has drawn earlier between values and goods, that is, between values and the empirical circumstances or situations with which they first become apparent.[2]

Just as he has previously argued that it is possible – indeed, necessary – to conceive of values independent from their empirical instantiations, Scheler here asserts that there must be a hierarchy of values which is itself distinct from any specific order of preference. 'The hierarchy of values (*Rangordnung der Werte*) is itself absolutely invariable, while the order of preference (*Vorzugsregeln*) in history is itself variable. . .' (FORM 106)

The distinction Scheler is attempting to mark here, between the value hierarchy and any particular order of value preference, may be clarified by expanding an analogy he draws between the latter – now characterised as a 'morality' – and a particular 'style' in art. (FORM 44–45) Just as any identifiable aesthetic style will exhibit a relatively fixed relationship between the constituents of art – consider, for example, the preoccupation with geometrical form that distinguishes cubism – so too any given morality will privilege one mode of values over others. Thus, by extension, we are able to describe various societies and cultures as 'materialistic', 'heroic' or 'spiritual' where we find them privileging the values of a hedonistic utilitarianism, of courage and self-sacrifice, or of a transcendent religious order. But, from this, Scheler does not draw the presumptive conclusion. In his view, this historical variation does not provide warrant for ethical relativism. On the contrary, such historical differences presuppose the necessity for an *invariable* hierarchy of values of which the former are modifications. Unless we have recourse to this invariable order there is no possibility of undertaking an axiological comparison of differing societies and cultures.

Here we find Scheler alluding once again to a prominent feature of our experience of values. As our immediate encounters with the world of our physical and social environment are rich with normative expressions and perceptions, so also our reflections on the past reveal preferences and judgements for and upon the respective merits of various periods in history. If, for example, I would defend a liking for the narrative of Periclean Athens over that of Carolingian France, I might find myself citing a preference for certain values (community, honour, glory and so on) that are present in both, but expressed more completely in the one instance than the other. Thus, whether the topic is the individual experience of values or their cultural manifestation, the message for Scheler is the same: whenever a value is given or expressed, the said value is assigned some status in a graded order of values.

This last claim marks one of Scheler's most significant and bold steps beyond Kant. With Kant, we are asked to settle for a very circumscribed moral alternative, to act or not to act solely on that maxim that we are able consistently to universalise. Yet, as often as not, we are faced with two alternative courses of action, each capable of being universalised in the Kantian sense. In such instances, the moral agent remains stranded on the reefs of Kant's formalism. As Nicolai Hartmann, along with a host of commentators on the Kantian ethics, has demonstrated by exploring the categorical imperative to never lie, Kant's unyielding commitment to truth-telling generates serious practical difficulties.

> There are situations which place before a man the inescapable alternative either of sinning against truthfulness or against some other equally high, or even some higher, value. A physician violates his professional duty if he tells a patient who is dangerously ill the critical state of his health; the imprisoned soldier who, when questioned by the enemy, allows the truth about his country's tactics to be extorted from him, is guilty of high treason; a friend, who does not try to conceal information given to him in strictest personal confidence, is guilty of breach of confidence. In all such cases the mere virtue of silence is not adequate. If the physician, the prisoner, the possessor of confidential information will do their duty of warding off a calamity that threatens, they must resort to a lie. But if they do so, they make themselves guilty on the side of truthfulness.[3]

Against these dilemmas, Scheler's insistence that we acknowledge the reality of a value hierarchy carries the possibility that the realisation of one value might be better than another and that knowledge of the normative order might be brought to bear upon the problem of their resolution. But, this claim is provisional, of course, upon Scheler's ability to demonstrate, not merely the possibility of a hierarchy of values, but the cognitive means whereby such a hierarchy might become instrumental in a philosophy of ethics. It is here where he makes his most ambitious claim for phenomenological intuition.

THE CRITERIA OF VALUATION

In chapter 3 we noted the eight *a priori* propositions Scheler attributes to a phenomenological intuition of the relationships between values. While these propositions enjoy the strength of any logically consistent statement, they do not speak directly to the content of our value experience. They are, in effect, the formal propositions of the material ethics of values. Hence, they tell us little of what we should or might choose when faced with the demands of conflicting norms. It is appropriate, then, if not necessary, for Scheler to flesh out his propositional structure with the following five criteria for determining the respective merits of competing values.

Scheler's first criterion speaks to the quality of permanence: the more enduring (*dauerhafter*) a value, the higher it is with respect to other values. In other words, the ability of a value to persist through time – to survive the vicissitudes of history, alterations in style and taste, and the trials of day to day existence – is one indication that it should be assigned a preferred status in any scale of values. As an example of how endurance stands as a measure and quality of values, Scheler offers 'love'. If, he asserts, I affirm my love for someone, I do not qualify my testimony by saying, 'I love you *now*', or otherwise indicate that this love is momentary. Rather, the notion of duration is conveyed in the affirmation itself. And if I find at some point that this love is gone, I must conclude that I misunderstood and misstated my original sentiment, that I never really loved this person. For genuine love would and must endure, in its own way as unstrained as the quality of mercy is for Shakespeare's Portia. 'Thus we arrive at a certain indication of how the criterion contributes to the "eminence" (*Hohe*) of a value. As the lowest value is at the same time the most transitory (*flüchtigsten*) the highest is the most eternal (*ewigen*). . . . But whether this criterion is also the original and intrinsic criterion for the eminence of a value is another question.' (FORM 110)

The second of Scheler's criteria entails the extent to which a value is diminished or consumed in its various expressions and manifestations. 'It is also certain that a value is higher the less it is divisible (*teilbar*) – that is, the less it must be divided as more and more (individuals) participate in it.' (FORM 110) The value of a loaf of bread – its material nutritive value – is divisible into a finite number of slices, and eventually exhausted in such division, while the value of a work of art (beauty) does not diminish with the frequency of its expressions, or, in Scheler's terms, its realisations.

Third, a value is higher *the less* it is dependent upon the existence of another value for its own worth. Thus, in the distinction between the values of utility and the values of such self-subsistent pleasures as those invoked by the passage of a calm and peaceful twilight, we would, or should, recognise the higher worth of the latter, since whatever value pertains to the former (for example, the value of a tool) is dependent upon the value it was designed to serve.[4]

As a fourth criterion Scheler cites the quality of satisfaction which the realisation of some values brings.

> As a criterion for value-eminence (*Werthöhe*) there is also the depth of satisfaction (*Teife der Befriedigung*) which accompanies our feeling (*Fühlen*) of it. While surely its eminence does not *subsist* in this 'depth of satisfaction' there is nevertheless an essential relationship between 'higher value' and 'deeper satisfaction'. What is meant here by 'satisfaction' has nothing to do with desire (*Lust*). . . . Satisfaction is an experience of fulfillment (*Erfüllungserlebnisse*). (FORM 113).

With this observation Scheler seems on the verge of sacrificing the independence and objectivity of values he so studiously seeks to affirm. For, despite his disclaimer that the eminence of a value does not subsist in the satisfaction it elicits, nonetheless by introducing an *essential* relationship between such eminence and satisfaction or feeling, Scheler would seem to give sensibility a *decisive* role in the structured ranking of values. It is one thing to claim, as we have seen him do, that our feelings and preferences suggest the possibility of some hierarchical arrangement between values. But it is quite another matter to make these feelings a criterion with which we might discover which values should be assigned a higher, or highest, position in such an arrangement.

Yet it would be misleading to belabour this point. We have already found him aware of the crucial distinction between subjective value preferences and the objective realm of values to which they refer. What is more, Scheler hastens to follow his discussion of *Befriedigung* with a caveat. 'But no matter how much these criteria for the superiority of values may be grounded in an essential relationship between values they are not able to give the ultimate sense (*letzen Sinn*) of this superiority.' (FORM 114) Here Scheler acknowledges that his first four criteria do not yield a conclusive standard by which we might assess the eminence of any given value. Rather, they serve only as intimations (much as *Vorziehen* has already done for the possibility of a normative order) of 'a deeper lying principle. . . through which we might be able to grasp the ultimate sense of this 'superiority' and from which the previously mentioned criteria might be derived'. (FORM 114)

What, then, is suggested with these earlier criteria? With the exception of the fourth, Scheler's arguments imply that those values least qualified or conditioned in their expression, or through their relationship with material objects, are the highest. It is not surprising, then, to find him proclaiming, as his fifth and decisive principle, that 'the essential characteristic (the most primordial characteristic) is that the "higher value" is the less relative value, the highest value is the "*absolute*" value. The other essential relationships are grounded in this'. (FORM 117)

It is crucial to note here that when Scheler speaks of the 'relativity' of values he does not have in mind that correspondence between values and subjectivity which characterises ethical relativism; that situation in which values might differ – exist or not exist – in accordance with the various prejudices, customs and tastes of individuals or cultures. Instead, he has in mind something far more fundamental, namely, the extent to which a value, by its very nature, presupposes or is contingent upon sensibility as such. In his formulation, the relativity which pertains to the value of pleasure does not stem from the fact that individuals find pleasure in different objects or circumstances but, rather, from the fact that pleasure is contingent upon the existence of *some* sensuous being (*sinnlich-fühlende Wesen*). Similarly, the values 'noble' and 'vulgar' are relative to the existence of some living-being (*Lebewesen*). Absolute values, on the other hand, are those which are not so contingent: those values which are not dependent upon the existence of any sensuous or living being but, instead, are the necessary correlate to the notion of feeling in general. (FORM 115)

As a minimal condition for understanding the intention of this extraordinary claim we must recall Scheler's phenomenology. Only within the context of the phenomenological reduction does it make sense to speak of values that do not presuppose the existence of a sensuous or living being. For it is only within such a philosophical setting that all questions of existence and non-existence are suspended. As his use of such constructions as *sinnlich-fühlende Wesen* and *Lebewesen* indicates, Scheler's reflections have finally reached the point where he is seeking to describe the *essential* content of the *consciousness* of values.[5]

But this will hardly suffice! Scheler's intention will remain ambiguous and imprecise until we have a clear idea of the distinction between sensible feeling and pure feeling, together with some understanding of what sort of subjectivity would correspond to each. If we are not to presuppose the existence of a sensible living being as the subjective correlate of absolute values, these values must have reference to *some* entity if Scheler is to realise his goal of achieving a bond between Man and the moral world. In my view, this clarification can best be accomplished by considering the typology of values Scheler develops from the above criteria.

THE HIERARCHY OF VALUES

As we would expect, the lowest rank in Scheler's scale of values is occupied by those which can be most simply described as 'sensible values', the values which fall within the range of what is agreeable or disagreeable to a sentient being. These are the values that correspond to the feeling states (*Gefühlszustande*) of pleasure and pain, enjoyment and suffering.

Here we are given an important clarification of the distinction Scheler wishes to mark between ethical relativism and his own understanding of the relationship which pertains between subjectivity and the nature of values. On the nature of sensible values, Scheler writes, 'this particular value-rank (*Wertreihe*) is relative to the Being of a sensible nature in general, but it is most certainly not relative to a particular organism, for example, a man, and also not relative to any specific thing or event which for the disposition (*Wesen*) of a particular organism might be agreeable or disagreeable'. (FORM 122) Thus, the relationship between sensible values and sensible nature belongs first within an *a priori* hierarchy of value modalities, and thereby takes precedence over any historical, cultural or individual expressions of preference or taste. For Scheler, it matters not what object or situation I might find pleasure in, what is significant is the fact that whatever circumstances or things promote my pleasure or provoke my displeasure derive their value through their intrinsic relationship to sensibility, itself understood as a material *a priori* condition. Similarly, the 'agreeable' will always be preferred over the 'disagreeable' despite the fact that individuals might differ markedly in what specific things or states promote the expression of either sentiment.

Here it is worth noting that, for Scheler, the demand to prefer the agreeable over the disagreeable does not bespeak a necessary *linguistic* truth. At issue is not the consistent employment of language but, rather, the fact that the consistent use of normative language, no less than the experience of values, is contingent upon the *phenomenological* reality of the relevant norms. As one recent commentary on this aspect of Scheler's thought notes, 'metaphysics is inescapable in some fashion. . . all knowledge, he claims, even knowledge of universals, must have its ultimate or radical source in the self-givenness of things in reality. . . Knowing is portrayed to be a genuinely positive reception of reality, and not merely treated as critical, analytic or synthetic'.[6]

Scheler's presentation of the first and lowest rank of value modalities provides a particularly telling instance of the extent to which his ethics reflects the influence of Kant. The hierarchy of values is an explicit elaboration of *a priori* states and concepts where we find Scheler, like Kant, carefully guarding against the introduction of any empirical or *a posteriori* considerations in order to preserve the universal and necessary character of the value hierarchy. As his argument proceeds, we shall find that there is an increasing affinity – despite Scheler's inclusion of such conditions as 'sensibility', 'feeling', and so on – between his understanding of the realm of values and that intelligible system of nature which, for Kant, stood under the autonomy of pure practical reason and the moral law.

One rank above sensible values stand the values of life (*Lebenswerte*), or the values which correspond to vital feelings (*vitalen Fühlens*). At the positive end of this value mode are the values of nobility (*Edlen*) while the negative pole comprises the values of the mean, the base, and the common (*Gemeinen*).[7] 'The terms "noble" and "base", however, are used here in their amoral or non-virtuous sense, equivalent to the German "*Tüchtigen*" and "*Schlectin*" that typically refer to physical states or well being or ill being.' (FORM 123) Hence, as examples of vital values Scheler cites health, disease, vigour, weakness and the like.

In making the distinction between vital and sensible values Scheler is anxious to avoid what he considers the fundamental error (*Grundgebrechen*) of utilitarianism and hedonism, namely, the reduction of all vital values to those states or objects which are either useful or agreeable. The source of this error, he claims, is the failure to recognise that 'life' is a distinct essence (*das Leben eine echte Wesenheit ist*) with its own intrinsic value, which cannot be reduced to the status of simply another attribute of the empirical organism. (FORM 124) My life, he is insisting, belongs to a distinctive order of value, quite different, and more precious, than my tastes, desires and preferences, all of which can be understood as the means which serve my pleasure.

Once again we find Scheler claiming *a priori* status for the conditions and categories of the value hierarchy. But there is in this latest point another feature which, although it receives little elaboration in the *Formalismus*, deserves mention. We have only to recall the work of John Stuart Mill to note that utilitarianism does, as Scheler claims, involve the reduction of life to the status of a means.

> The creed which accepts as the foundation of morals, Utility, or the Greatest Happiness Principle, holds that actions are right in proportion as they tend to promote happiness, wrong as they tend to produce the reverse of happiness. By happiness is intended pleasure, the absence of pain; by unhappiness, pain, and the privation of pleasure. To give a clear view of the moral standard set up by the theory, much more requires to be said; in particular, what things it includes in the ideas of pain and pleasure; and to what extent this is left an open question. But these supplementary explanations do not affect the theory of life on which this theory of morality is grounded – namely, *that pleasure, and freedom from pain, are the only things desirable as ends*; and that all desirable things (which are as numerous in the utilitarian as in any other scheme) are desirable either for the pleasure inherent in themselves, or as means to the promotion of pleasure and the prevention of pain.[8] (my emphasis)

Scheler's insistence upon the autonomy (*selbständigkeit*) of life and the values relative to it does much to preserve the meaning and worth of life as an end in itself. What is more, by carefully delineating the sensible values (pleasure and pain) from other values, he manages to avoid many of the difficulties Mill encounters in seeking to define the true nature of pleasure, difficulties G. E. Moore makes much of in his *Principia Ethica*.[9]

Nonetheless, despite the analytic importance of the distinction between sensible values and vital values, both are, as we have seen, relative to the idea of a living-sensuous Being. As such, all of the values that fall within these two modalities of value occupy an inferior position in Scheler's hierarchy. Care, then, must be taken to distinguish between them and the two latter modalities, the spiritual and the holy.

In his exposition of spiritual values Scheler writes,

The acts and functions in which we comprehend them are functions of spiritual feelings and acts of spiritual preferences, loves, and hates. . . The principle types (*Hauptarten*) of these values are: 1) the values of 'beauty' (*Schön*) and 'the ugly' (*Hässlich*) and the whole domain of pure aesthetic values; 2) the values of 'right' (*Rechten*) and 'wrong' (*Unrechten*). . . which constitute the foundation for all legal orders. . . and 3) the values of pure cognition of the truth (*der reinen Wahreitserkenntnis*) which – in distinction from that knowledge of the positive sciences that has as its goal the domination of natural phenomena (*Beherrschung der Erscheinungen*) – philosophy seeks to realise. (FORM 124, 125)

One distinctive feature of this value mode is, according to Scheler, the fact that spiritual values subsist independently of any changes in the sphere of vital values. In fact, the cognition of spiritual values does not even presuppose the mediation of a physical subject or an ego. Instead, these values are given immediately in spiritual feelings. (FORM 125)

Despite the somewhat tortured, and seemingly preposterous, character of Scheler's discussion, the situation he describes is not far removed from ordinary experience. When we are in the presence of what we experience as great art, or when our reflections lead us to the realisation of some deep and lasting insight, all of our common and mundane concerns – the physical as well as the mental – are suspended as consciousness is consumed or absorbed in the presence of its object. Scheler's claim that the ego is not an essential element in the cognition of spiritual values seems to be substantiated by the fact that as we come to give our *selves* over to the work of a Beethoven, a Michelangelo, Van Gogh, or Aristotle we reach a different level of understanding and sensitivity. But, if the ego is not implicated in such 'spiritual' feelings, the object of these feelings (spiritual values) must still have some referent in subjectivity: it is still the case that we are moved, touched, and 'carried away' in the experience of beauty and the perception of life's deepest meanings.

It is here in the unfolding of Scheler's ethics that we begin to glimpse the pivotal role 'the Person' will subsequently play. For it is the *Person*, in distinction from the psycho-physical ego, which stands as the corollary of all spiritual acts and the values realised in such acts.[10] This, then, is the direction Scheler will take to resolve the difficulty we encountered earlier (see p.75 above), namely, the problem of establishing the kind or mode of Being which corresponds to absolute values.

The relationship between the highest values and the Person is rendered more explicitly when Scheler takes up with the fourth rank of values. Those values that constitute the sphere of 'the holy' and 'the unholy' – *die Heilege* and *die Unheilege* – are, in his formulation, legitimately and essentially (*Wesensgesetzmassig*) values of the Person (*Personwerte*). (FORM 126) Scheler deliberately eschews any definitive account of this modality of values, preferring to rest with the observation that they are given only in the appearance of absolute objects (*absolute Gegenstände*). (FORM 125) However, with his insistence that this modality of values is independent of anything that has been deemed holy by any people at any time, he signals his desire to reserve the positive expressions of this realm of values for the intuition of pure and absolute objects of being itself.[11]

THE VALUE HIERARCHY APPRAISED

As the preceding discussion indicates, Scheler's enunciation of the value hierarchy is a bit more sketchy than we would wish. Nonetheless, his comments deserve some consideration, if only because they represent one of the few systematic attempts in modernity to provide philosophical justification for the traditional

values of Western civilisation: to affirm the supremacy of the
beautiful, the true, and the abiding over the faddish, the expedi-
ent, and ephemeral affairs that have become a preoccupation
throughout so much of our culture.

In my judgement, there can be little criticism, beyond that I
have already made, of the manner in which Scheler applies his
criteria to the content of our value experience. Once we accept
his assertion that the higher values are those least contingent upon
the sensibility of any individual or collectivity, his development
of the hierarchy follows quite consistently. But, what grounds
do we have for accepting these criteria? We have seen that
Scheler's reply is, in effect, 'none, save those given in intuition'.
In commenting on the fifth criterion, which asserts that the less
relative a value, the higher it is, he observes that strict attention
to procedures of comparison or induction tends to conceal more
than it reveals about the relative or absolute character of any given
value. Prior to the employment of any such procedures, 'there
is a profundity (*Teife*) in us whereby we always know secretly
(*wo wir immer heimlich wissen*) the relativity an experienced value
has for a given state of affairs'. (FORM 116) As instances of this
deeper level of cognition Scheler cites the examples of Socrates,
'who *knew* "that he knew nothing" but who secretly understood
that the moral to be drawn from this was that "his values were
not absolute values" ', and Christ, who said ' "no man is good",
feeling in his perception of absolute values that no man is the
bearer of good, except God'. (FORM 116–117)

This appeal to a deeper, intuitive, level of normative cognition
is present again when Scheler writes of the value hierarchy itself.
'It is hereafter clear that the hierarchy of values can never be
deduced or derived. Whichever value is higher is always grasped
in an act of preference or depreciation. There is for this an
intuitive preferential-evidence (*Vorzugsevidenz*) that is in no way
supplemented by logical deduction.' (FORM 107)

We were prepared early on in this study for this turn in Scheler's
thought by his sympathetic references to Pascal and the *logique
de coeur*, as well as by his initial attempts to demonstrate how
phenomenology can expand the field of inquiry that is accessible
to intuitive knowledge. However, we have also noted the extent
to which he was prone to make unwarranted claims for such
intuition, the tendency of phenomenology to render any ontic
distinctions between form and matter meaningless, and, as I

have been suggesting, Scheler's inability to free himself from the presuppositions of Kant's ethics. It is to these three factors that we can, in my estimation, attribute most of the failings and difficulties we encounter with Scheler's value hierarchy.

First, Scheler's exclusive appeal to intuition precludes the development of any perspective or method that would compel us to accept his criteria as axiomatic, and thus there is no imperative for choosing to express, or realise, those values he affirms as the absolute and the highest. We are given no detailed presentation of the steps through which he arrives at his conclusions, no reflection upon the relationship between his criteria (we have, for example, observed that the fourth criterion is not altogether consistent with the others), and no means whereby we might rationally criticise the evidence and claims of another's intuition. Lacking the latter, there can be no discursive and rational resolution of any disagreement between Scheler and the individual who claims to know intuitively that the values of life are supreme and that whenever there is a conflict, the values of beauty, religion, and philosophy must become subordinate or, if need be, sacrificed altogether. Lacking some attention to these genuine considerations, considerations which any moral philosophy must be able to address, Scheler's ethics tends to remain an account of one man's normative experience.

This is not to imply that the hierarchy of values and the criteria on which they are based are insignificant. On the contrary, they are, as is the work of any sensitive and seminal thinker, challenging and enlightening. But Scheler intends more. At one point he makes the claim that a distinctive feature of spiritual values is that the vital values ought to be 'sacrificed' for them, thereby giving clear indication of his intention to make his value schema binding for ethical choices. (FORM 124) Yet, unless he offers some formal principle, akin to Kant's criterion of universality, by which we might test the morality of a given act, Scheler's 'ought' has neither the rationale nor the logical force of Kant's categorical imperative.

This difficulty might be vitiated were it not for the second factor, namely, the tendency of Scheler's phenomenology to dissolve any ontological distinctions between the formal and the material constituents of value experience. We have already noted this disposition in the previous chapter, where I reflected on the problems which might ensue from Scheler's 'materialist reduction'. Now we are able to consider the ramifications of this reduction in more detail.

If, as Scheler contends, all the content of value experience – the objects of our particular preferences as well as the values of beauty, truth, and so on – enjoy the status of material *a priori* facts, in and through phenomenological intuition, then it is impossible for Scheler to argue that the material of such sensibility and feeling can be introduced into morality without denying morality any critical and practical force. We can, as he has shown, make universal and necessary judgements *vis-à-vis* these phenomena, for example, that preference inevitably implies a graded order of values. However, with phenomenology, material events and objects are given *a priori* status only through a process which suspends and neutralises the distinctions and assumptions – for example, the naturalistic thesis – that infuse our real experience.[12] Thus, Scheler's desire to maintain essential and unique distinctions between the various objects of value experience, within the context of the phenomenological *epoche*, would seem to violate the letter, if not the spirit, of the phenomenological philosophy and method.

For example, his contentions that spiritual values are more absolute than vital values, and that there is a necessary correlation between absolute values and the Person, introduces ontological nuances and relationships which are extrinsic to the phenomenological realm, rigidly understood. As Husserl points out,

> a phenomenon. . . is no 'substantial' unity; it has no 'real properties', it knows no real parts, no real changes, and no causality; all these words are here understood in the sense proper to natural science. To attribute a nature to phenomena, to investigate their real component parts, their causal connections – that is pure absurdity, no better than if one wanted to ask about the casual properties, connections, etc., of numbers. It is the absurdity of naturalizing something whose essence excludes the kind of being that nature has.[13]

If I read Husserl correctly, we may say that once all distinctions between imaginary, illusory, and real being – and between the formal and material elements of experience – are suspended in favour of a common designation of the phenomena as material *a priori* essents (*Wesenheit*), then the distinctions Scheler is trying to preserve (for example, between absolute and relative values) must also be suspended.

We have seen other indications that Scheler's employment of the phenomenological method is less consistent than one would expect. His claim that philosophical knowledge is of a higher value than applied knowledge is, as it stands, an uncritical wedding of Platonism and phenomenology. Similarly, his distinction between sensible and pure feelings, with the latter defined as those that do not presuppose the existence of a sensible being, is an appropriation of the traditional division of the psyche into two distinct types of activity; thought, which is independent of sensory perception, and sensibility, which is contingent upon the mediation of the body.

All of these criticisms are well summarised in an observation Herbert Speigelberg offers on Scheler's employment of the phenomenological method.

> ... not all of his discoveries and insights seem to be sufficiently underpinned. Many of them were apparently not yet exposed to the cleansing fire of critical doubt and to the attempt to think through alternative perspectives and interpretations. Scheler was too often in a hurry. Phenomenology was for him only a stepping stone on the way to his ulterior objectives. In the dazzling outpouring of his overflowing mind he was too prone to mistake his first flashes for final insights. This often led him to make excessive claims for his final conclusions as based upon phenomenological evidence, almost in inverse proportion to the care he spent in testing them.[14]

Spiegelberg suggests, and I concur, that any attempt to read Scheler's ethics as an exercise in phenomenology is of limited value. Once we proceed beyond the negative or critical themes in the *Formalismus* – those themes where he takes up with the weaknesses of ethical formalism and, to a lesser degree, of utilitarianism and hedonism – the confusions and inconsistencies we encounter are simply too disconcerting.

SCHELER'S 'TRANSCENDENTAL OBJECTIVISM'

How then, are we to take Scheler? In my view, Manfred Fring's characterisation of the *materiale Wertethik* as 'an emotional transcendental objectivism' comes much closer to expressing the spirit and tenor of Scheler's work than any other designation.[15] This designation serves to capture the kinship between Scheler and Kant we have observed throughout this study, as well as lending a degree of credence to the value hierarchy that is lacking when we view that order solely as the creature of an exercise in phenomenology. For example, Scheler's postulation of the hierarchy of values exemplifies, in significant measure, the type of proof that Norman Kemp Smith attributed to Kant. (See the discussion of *Wille* and *Willkür* in chapter 2.) The obvious difference from Kant is, however, that Scheler takes *Vorziehen* as his given point of departure and then seeks to elaborate those 'transcendental' features which are the universal and necessary conditions that stand as the antecedent conditions of *Vorziehen* and the feelings derived from it.

Once we adopt the suggestion that each of the notions which Scheler articulates in his value hierarchy has this transcendental character – that is, are akin to those concepts in the Kantian philosophy which are not reducible to experience but are, nonetheless, necessary if experience is to be brought within the province of knowledge[16] – many of the problems we have noted are softened, if not altogether resolved. The entire hierarchy of values is now cast in the mode of a transcendental realism whose various levels and modes are the necessary correlate to differing degrees of preference and feeling. The 'agreeable', the 'vital', the 'beautiful', and the 'eternal' are the objective counterpart of four discrete emotional states. But, lest we introduce a derived and unwarranted set of new problems, it must be clear that by characterising the value modalities as objective we do not assign them a reality independent of any normative acts of preference, willing or feeling. Rather, the term 'objective' here is intended to convey Scheler's conviction that, as Frings points out, 'the emotional *a priori* givenness of values and their ranks does not follow subjective, social or historical factors. . .'[17]

An important feature of this interpretation is that it tends to diminish the arbitrary character of Scheler's distinction between relative and absolute values. Within such a transcendental framework it is possible to introduce those ontic distinctions that a strict application of the phenomenological method will not allow. We have, for example, seen Kant, with his distinction between a system of empirical nature and a system of intelligible nature, introducing the possibility of postulating a relative and an absolute ontological realm, each displaying its respective transcendental concepts and categories. The law of causality, in this reading, is one such instance of a transcendental concept contingent upon, or relative, to sensibility; freedom, in contrast, stands as an instance of a transcendental concept that necessarily implies the notion of an absolute and pure mode of being, namely, the autonomous will.

At this point it is important to observe that, once again, the extent to which Scheler's contention that values are higher the less they are conditioned by their relationship to sensibility is made in the spirit of Kant's effort to purge ethics of any particularly subjective or empirical conditions. However, the attempt to interpret Scheler's ethics from the perspective of a transcendental philosophy will be premature until we have explored the matter of whether or not other key elements in this ethics display similar transcendental implications. In particular, it is not enough to consider the values that stand as the objective correlates to the various emotional states: we must also inquire into the nature of that entity which stands as the bearer (*Träger*) of these states, namely the Person. Further, if we are to pursue and complete the theme of philosophical kinship that binds Scheler to Kant, we must also determine whether the concept of the Person functions in the *materiale Wertethik* as it does in the second Critique, that is, as the locus of all specifically *moral* acts. These are the themes which will occupy much of our attention in chapter 5.

5
The Person

Max Scheler's philosophy of the Person comprises the major portion of Part Two of the *Formalismus* and was written some three years after he completed the first part of his treatise on ethics. While there can be little doubt that the two sections deserve inclusion in one study – from the very outset he insisted that this work be characterised as an ethical personalism – we should be aware of some significant differences between the approach in Part One and the way Scheler treats the subject matter of Part Two. Most striking is the fact that in Part Two Scheler makes little effort to justify his arguments and assertions through an appeal to phenomenology. 'Although this doctrine' (of the Person) 'forms the climax of his magnum opus, and the center of his philosophy, I can see comparatively little phenomenological foundation for it, especially since Scheler does little if anything to justify his sweeping and often astonishing pronouncements in this area.'[1]

This assessment of Herbert Speigelberg ought not cause us undue distress. While Scheler certainly does depart from the context of phenomenology that flavoured his earlier reflections, we will find that his philosophy of the Person is both seminal and insightful. To be sure, his approach in Part Two is even more didactic and expository than in those areas we have already dealt with. But in many respects this is a refreshing development. Part Two is replete with the rich illustrations and examples that are notably absent from the earlier sections of the *Formalismus*. More significantly, perhaps, the reader is no longer forced to discriminate within each of Scheler's presentations in an attempt to isolate those features which are purely speculative from those which are the result of legitimate phenomenological analysis. Instead we can summarise his observations with a view towards assessing their consistency, delineating the gist of his vision and, finally (as we have previously done in brief fashion with Kant) exploring the implications of Scheler's personalism for our understanding of the human condition.

THE TRANSCENDENTAL DEDUCTION OF THE PERSON

As Scheler begins his commentary he again reaches back to delineate the Kantian position, once more feeling the need to cast his own formulations in the reflecting light of Kant's thought. In formal ethics, he writes, the Person is characterised only as rational Person (*Vernunftperson*). This, Scheler observes, is the necessary consequence of the fact that in formalism all the material of willing, and thereby all the content of morality, has been excised. The most that can then be said of the Person is that it has the status of a logical 'x' that must be presupposed as the point of departure for every act of will. (FORM 370–371) While this approach is not without some merit – it does, for example, preclude the possibility of treating the Person as a thing or object – its general thrust, Scheler argues, is to reduce the moral status of Man to that of a *homo logos* or *homo noumenon*. The result, therefore, is to strip human beings of their unique dignity, for once Kant opposes the idea of the Person to phenomenal Man, the Person is assigned the status of a thing-in-itself within Kant's system, indistinguishable from any other thing-in-itself. (FORM 373)

Here Scheler is very briefly summarising the discourse we traced in chapter 2 of this study. There we observed Kant positing the Person and personality as two necessary implications of the moral law. Insofar as this argument took the form of a transcendental deduction – with the Person emerging as one of the necessary conditions that render our experience of the moral law possible – there is clearly merit in Scheler's contention that in Kant's philosophy the Person serves as a merely logical principle of Reason. However, when Scheler proceeds to assert that the Person is, as a noumenal concept in Kant, indistinguishable from any other thing-in-itself, he is ignoring the central message of the second *Critique*; namely, that our experience of the moral law, or 'ought', enables thought to gain access to the noumenal realm and to speak with assurance of those transcendental concepts that Reason employs in its *practical* capacity. To be sure, the fact that Kant is dealing with practical Reason imposes some strictures upon the range of our inferences: we are thereby entitled to treat only those concepts – freedom, the moral will, and personality – that are given as necessary and universal conditions for the moral law, and then, only to deal with these concepts as principles in an intelligible system of nature. But an intelligible principle is (at least in this instance) something far different from the unknowable *ding-an-sich* that stands beyond the bounds of sensibility in the *Critique of Pure Reason*. What is more, we have previously noted Kant's contention that the idea of personality commands our highest respect, a claim that would be absurd if the Person were the indistinguishable cipher that Scheler's criticism implies.

How could Scheler be guilty of such a distortion, and apparent misinterpretation of Kant? The answer, in my judgement, lies in his twofold concern to address the fullness of our normative experience and to do so concretely; a project he has repeatedly posed as the sorely needed complement to the austerely rationalist approach of ethical formalism. In the present context, his intentions are revealed in his underscored assertions that *'Person is the concrete self-subsistent unity of acts of a diversified nature'*, and that *'the Being of the Person founds all essentially different acts'*. (FORM 382, 383) At issue here is Scheler's insistence that the Person does not appear as the necessary correlate of any specific human activity–such as thinking, willing, loving, hating, and so on – but, rather, must be understood as that entity which unifies modes of activity that, as we have seen, have their own distinctive and essential places within the hierarchy of values.

These considerations rest on the premises that there is a qualitative difference between the various modes of normative experience and activity. Unless we presuppose some unifying agency there are no grounds for claiming that the same being is involved in all these expressions of valuation. At first reading this claim seems obvious, so obvious as to be almost trivial. But the matter is somewhat less so if we recall the sharp distinction Kant ultimately drew between those actions that are sentient and those which are purely rational. Scheler's remarks become more meaningful yet, when we further recall the difficulties between actions that are subject to natural determination and those which presuppose causality through freedom. Thus, when Scheler insists that we must posit some principle that embraces all acts and modes of valuation, he makes a significant move towards healing the Kantian diremption between phenomenal and noumenal Man.

However, there is much more at issue here than the articulation of some *principle* of unity. With his repeated characterisations of the Person as concrete, Scheler is attempting to bring the Person out of the realm of philosophical abstraction and onto the stage of human practice. The Person, he writes, 'is and experiences itself only as act-consummating being (*actvollziehendes Wesen*) and in no sense is behind or above those acts, like a static point (*ein ruhender Punct*) which stands over the accomplishing or achieving of its acts'. (FORM 384) Furthermore, the whole Person is involved in each of its acts and, in a non-temporal manner, varies with each such act. The identity of the Person, then, consists only in the qualitative direction of its becoming different (*Anderswerden*) with the result that, if we are to locate the Person, we must look beyond every experience which is manifest or apparent to us towards the being which is *having* that experience.[2] (FORM 385) With this approach Scheler invites us to become sensitive to the whole panorama of human expression. For it is the qualitative peculiarity of *how* the Person acts which accounts for the variety and differences between Persons. (FORM 385–386)

The image that these remarkable assertions evoke is that of a continuous self-transcendence. The whole of personality is brought to bear upon each new expression or act of the individual, not as some constant or indeterminant structure, but as a fluid existence in a state of dynamic interaction with itself, insofar as it is constantly modified and expanded through and by its own actions. If we allow our imaginations to run over the incredible complexity this process involves in any given individual, we can begin to appreciate the nearly infinite complexity of normative expressions the human species exhibits. Whether we consider Man as a social, an artistic, or a spiritual being the range of possible communal, creative and loving expressions and experiences would seem to be boundless.

It is important to observe here that by locating the Person at the centre of all acts of valuation, Scheler honours Kant's dictum that, as neither substance nor thing, the Person can never be treated as an object without doing violence to its elemental nature. 'The nature of the Person is never objective. . . The single and exclusive manner in which it expresses itself is, on the contrary, only in the execution of its acts (or in the execution of a reflection upon its acts. . .' (FORM 386) What is more, it would seem from this discussion that, with respect to his reflections on the nature of the Person, Scheler does indeed fulfil his ambition to flesh out the skeletal conception drawn by Kant.

However, we cannot move beyond these introductory passages on Scheler's conceptualisation of the Person without considering whether his remarks have anything more to commend them than the richness of their texture and the bold intellectual horizons they envision. Are, then, these assertions grounded in a philosophical argument or simply part of a speculative, and somewhat fanciful, narrative? I think one can make a case for the former proposition on the premiss that Scheler's personalism is arrived at by means of a transcendental deduction that is, in its broader strokes and at its most crucial points, not unlike those of Kant.

We have seen (most explicitly in the 'Note on Method' in chapter 2) that one of the distinguishing features of Kant's transcendental deductions is their original and naïve acceptance of some experience or fact – for instance, sense experience or the moral law – and their subsequent elaboration of the conditions that render such experience possible. Scheler is following the same course when he writes that it is the Person that accounts for, and guarantees, the obvious unity we discern between acts that are in themselves essentially different. Here it is the experience of this unity that serves as the initial and provocative step in the deduction and which moves him to seek out what are, in effect, the 'enabling conditions' of such experience. The subsequent disclosing and articulation of the Person as that being whose nature is to serve as the unifying ground of all acts is, then, the concluding step in the deduction. This same process unfolds when Scheler asserts that we must presuppose the existence of the Person to account for our experience that one and the same individual is engaged in the disparate acts of loving, willing, desiring and so on. All this without, of course, being exhausted or consumed in, with, or by, any of them. In sum, the Person (or better, 'personality') is that universal and necessary ontological condition which grounds our experience of ourselves and others as integrated human beings.

In retrospect, it is difficult to conceive of Scheler disclosing the Person in any other way. For when he concludes that the Person is not a substance or entity that exists independently of its acts, he precludes the possibility of ever knowing the Person other than through the cognition of its acts. If the situation were otherwise, then Scheler would have to admit that it is possible to conceive of the Person apart from its active expressions, a possibility that would contradict the definition of the Person as that being which exists only in the execution of its acts and is given to us only through such acts.

In the end, one can only speculate on the reasons Scheler does not explicitly characterise his argument as a transcendental deduction. Stephen Schneck offers a plausible interpretation by suggesting an affinity between Scheler's personalism and the later work of Jürgen Habermas. Correctly citing Habermas's attempt to identify quasi-transcendental criteria – a technical, a practical and a critical interest that are constitutive of knowledge – 'by which social and political critique might be facilitated', Schneck further notes Habermas's insistence that these do not have independent existence but are located within human anthropology.[3] In this reading Scheler's concept of the Person is firmly grounded in the human condition, indeed the Person becomes a condition for any moral sense of humanity, rather than occupying a place in some metaphysical or idealist scheme.

To be sure, we are left with the absence of any firm support for such an interpretation by Scheler's reluctance to affiliate himself with the transcendental project. This reluctance, I am suggesting, stems from the misunderstanding of Kant we have noted earlier in this chapter. For if one fails to mark any distinction in Kant between a transcendental principle of Reason, a noumena, and the thing-in-itself, it is possible to suppose that all three share the unknowable and obscure character that, in fact, Kant attributes only to the thing-in-itself. The result is then a prejudice against any transcendental features which might insinuate themselves into one's philosophy. But, whatever Scheler's motives for avoiding the lexicon of the transcendental and critical philosophy, there seems little doubt that his presentation can be meaningfully interpreted within the context of a transcendental deduction. Moreover, our subsequent discussion will show that as Scheler's conception of the Person unfolds it acquires other attributes which can best be described as transcendental. This will be particularly true when we come to inquire further into the ontological status of the Person.

THE PERSON AND MORALITY

In the previous chapter we considered Scheler's philosophy of values at some length, without ever dwelling in any detail on the nature of the expressly moral values, good and evil. This omission was neither due to an oversight nor a failure on Scheler's part to treat these issues. Rather, it is my view that any adequate presentation of his understanding of good and evil can only come after we have clarified what he intends with his insistence that the Person is the centre of all normative acts. Having done so, we are now able to take up with the specific moral implications of his personalism.

Early on in the *Formalismus* Scheler indicates that the peculiar feature of good and evil is found in the fact that these values do not pertain to the objects or material of the will, but, instead, to the act of willing itself. 'The value good appears when we realise a higher positive value (which is given in preference); good appears *in* the act of willing. It is found, so to speak, on the back (*auf dem Rücken*) of these acts. . .' (FORM 48) With this reference to the material of the act of willing, Scheler has in mind those values which comprise the hierarchy of values. Thus, 'the value "good" – in an absolute sense – is that value which appears with the act of realising the highest value; the value "evil" – in an absolute sense – is that which appears with the act of realising the lowest value'. (FORM 47)

Scheler is aware that there is a strong echo of Kant in these claims, and he cites, as precedent for his position, Kant's contention that good and evil 'are properly referred to actions, not to the sensations of the Person, and if anything is to be good and evil absolutely (that is, in every respect and without any further condition, or is to be so esteemed, it can only be the manner of acting, the maxim of the will, and consequently the acting person himself as a good or evil man that can be so called, and not a thing'.[4] However, as we would expect, in Scheler's judgement this formulation has the effect of unduly restricting the province of good and evil to those acts that only bespeak the legality or illegality of the moral command or 'ought'. As such, it reduces the value of the Person to a secondary status, by making it a consequence of the value of willing – of whether or not the act conforms to the moral law – rather than recognising that this value ultimately rests upon and is grounded in the value of the Person. (FORM 49–51) Thus, Scheler insists that considerations of good and evil can and must take us to the core of all the Person's normative activity, rather than to a unilateral consideration of whether or not the will is in conformity with the moral law.

This crucial modification of Kant clearly anticipates Scheler's assertion that it is being of the Person that sustains all acts. Any analysis of acts must, for him, invoke the presence of the Person. To the extent that Kant would engage in a lengthy analysis of the act of willing, while only considering the being who wills subsequent to that analysis, he is reversing the actual relationship which obtains between Person and willing. But, there is more implied in Scheler's criticism. If the Person is the bearer of acts then the values good and evil are not *ultimately* features of acts, they are qualities of the Person. Hence, 'what can only be called good and evil originally. . . is the Person, the *being* of the Person itself, so that we can say without further ado; from the standpoint of the bearer: *good and evil are values of the Person (Personwerte)*. (FORM 49)

This assertion has the twofold virtue of grounding moral values *in* the person while ensuring the moral status *of* the Person. If good and evil were solely features of acts, then these attributes would be thereby removed from the acting agent and we would have difficulty conceiving how human beings might be said to be intrinsically and essentially moral agents. As I read Scheler, he is concerned here lest such an interpretation result in an extreme ethical behaviourism whereby all moral insights and judgements would be restricted to states of activity, rather than to states of human being. Consequently, any attempts or claims to assess the responsibility or merit of the individual would be philosophically unjustified. All that one could legitimately say would be that the act, rather than the actor, was good or evil. (This is what any ethics of virtues risks when it seeks to establish that the appropriate place for ethical considerations lies within or 'ingredient' to practices.[5]) Conversely, once the Person is taken as the ultimate locus of morality, it becomes something more than an entity which appears only with and in acts; the Person becomes, in effect a moral (but never an objective) substance, and personality a moral quality, of the human being.

This interpretation of Scheler's intent has the further merit of resolving a question that could easily be raised by a literal reading of his initial characterisation of the Person's relationship to its acts, namely, the matter of what becomes of the Person in the absence of normative activity? If it were the case that the Person is given completely in its acts, then the existence of the Person would be as ephemeral and fleeting as those gestures and acts which present themselves to the perceptions of others, like the poor player of Shakespeare's Macbeth who 'struts and frets his hour upon the stage and then is heard no more'. To be sure,

Scheler claims that the Person is not exhausted in its acts, but this claim seems at odds with his other observations to the effect that the Person is only present in its acts. Only if we conceive of the Person as the agential substance of all morality can we arrive at the notion of a mode of being that is present in its immediate acts while also persisting concurrently with the pattern or moral disposition that develops with, and emerges from, such acts. Thus, we are able to discern within the mosaic of their words and deeds, the quality of the Person – or the personality of a Jesus, a Socrates, a Mother Theresa or a Martin Luther King.

Nonetheless, not all the problems raised by Scheler's account of good and evil are so readily dispensed with. When he makes goodness a feature of those acts that realise the highest and positive values while designating as 'evil' those which realise the lowest and negative values, he seems to be compromising his conception of the Person with the same difficulties that marked his attempt to develop a hierarchy of values. If, for example, the pure and absolute good act is that which entails the realisation of the highest value, then the only truly good person would be the holy man. Similarly, if evil involves the choice of a lower value, would not the individual faced with the alternative of acting to realise the values of religion or those of the spirit – of becoming a priest or an artist – and subsequently opting for the latter, be choosing, in some sense, evil?

This problem is obviated to some extent by Scheler's willingness to entertain expressions of relative good and evil within the context of choices made *within* any given mode of values. (FORM 47) Presumably the choice to express or willfully *act* upon a preference for the beautiful over the ugly, rather than simply *feel* such a preference would, in Scheler's term, entail the 'appearance' of the good, while the will to express the ugly over the beautiful would be accompanied by the appearance of evil. But this acknowledgement of relative states of good and evil occurs in a very preliminary account. When we consider the question of good and evil in the light of his subsequent development of the hierarchy of values, the problem of an exclusive and absolutist account of the moral choices to be made when confronting alternatives *between* the various value modes haunts Scheler's depiction of personalist morality.

As we have seen, Scheler makes the will to sacrifice vital values for spiritual values an index of the higher station of spiritual values in his normative typology. (FORM 124) In so doing, the morality or goodness of the individual whose personality is expressed in the choice of life over death (both aspects of vital values) is somehow diminished in relation to those 'higher' types who choose to express the values of philosophical contemplation, artistic creation or love of the holy. (FORM 124) If this is the case then it would seem that a choice between good and evil is at issue in the realisation of values between the respective modes of value as well as within each mode. And that here, in any conflict between a higher and a lower mode, the alternative is, indeed, between the expression of good and the expression of evil.

In this setting a related, and deeper difficulty resurfaces, namely, the matter of establishing any grounds upon which one might assert that an individual ought to strive to become a good Person. In a discussion that is so subtle as to verge on the incomprehensible, Scheler is content with drawing a series of extremely fine distinctions between the various types of 'ought', that is, the 'ideal ought' and the 'normative ought' – while deliberately avoiding the articulation of any practical principles that might help us to determine how or whether to choose between contending values. (FORM 211–245)

It would be misleading to suggest that Scheler is ever able to resolve the problems that beset his ethics when one tries to bring the philosophy of values to bear upon his philosophy of the Person. Despite the many ways in which the hierarchy of values and personalism draw upon one another, there is an irreducible asymmetry between them that defines a distinctive tension in his thought. On the one hand, Scheler is unreleting in his attempts to pursue every nuance and distinction which arises from his detailed explication of the experience and the perception of values. For example, in a lengthy essay entitled *Vorbilder und Führer* ('models' and 'leaders') he develops a typology of personal archetypes that roughly corresponds to the various stages of the value hierarchy. But, as he pursues this theme he comes to identify five such archetypes (*Vorbildsmodelle*) – the artist of life (*Lebenskünstler*, the guiding spirit of a civilisation (*führenden Geist der Zivilisation*), the hero, the genius and the saint – while there are only four distinct ranks or modes of values.[6]

The other pole of the tension in Scheler's thought, and the one of greatest interest in this study, is found in his attempt to develop an increasingly exhaustive concept of the Person, one that will embrace and unify more and more dimensions of human experience. The culmination of this effort occurs with his discussion of the 'total man' in his *Philosophical Perspectives*[7]. We should not expect to find any reconciliation of these two themes. But, as I hope to indicate below, we must acknowledge that the tension they generate is a creative one which enables us to think afresh about some familiar themes and problems in political philosophy and theory.

INDIVIDUAL AND COLLECTIVE PERSON

As Scheler develops his expanded conception of the Person, some of its more insightful consequences and expressions come with his elaboration of the collective and individual dimensions of personality. The reader should be forewarned that these reflections include some of the more complex and nuanced distinctions that we encounter in the *Formalismus*. But, difficult as it might be, a careful reading of these passages is well worth the effort. Here Scheler's personalism will provide students familiar with the study of mass movements, liberalism, and conservatism a series of alternative perspectives that are both substantive and sensitive to some of the deeper problems encountered in the theory and practice of these social phenomena.

Scheler commences his reflections with the claim that 'the actual collective content (*Gesamtgehalt*) of all experiences that take the form of living with another (*Miteinanderlebens*). . . is the world of a community, a so-called collective world (*Gesamtwelt*) that has as its concrete acting subject a collective social Person'. In contrast, 'the active content for all experiences that take the form of singular acts and private experiences (*Fürsicherlebens*) is the world of an individual or an individual world (*Einzelwelt*), and its concrete acting subject is the individual Person'. (FORM 511)

After making this distinction Scheler hastens to note that it does not signify two different entities but, rather, describes a difference that can and should be made in any full or 'worldly' account of what is involved in being human. 'For every finite Person (*endlichen Person*) there is thus an individual Person (*Einzelperson*) and a collective Person (*Gesamtperson*); each necessary and essential (*wesensnotwendige*) sides of a concrete whole which comprises

Person and world'. (FORM 511)

Here it is imperative that we not be misled into the assumption that the collective Person represents the sum of individuals acting in a communal or social capacity. Nor is it the case that the will and content of the collective Person is reducible to, or wholly present, in the acts, values and intentions of its members. Yet, Scheler continues to insist that the collective Person is an aspect of the finite Person. (FORM 512)

The way towards an unravelling of these extremely complex formulations lies in Scheler's use of the term *wesensnotwendige.* Once again his thought seems to be taking a transcendental turn in order to describe those conditions that can account for a unique and irreducible feature of human experience. In the present instance he is concerned to provide room in his personalist philosophical anthropology for those experiences which invoke, in their very essence, the existence of others. Typically, Scheler eschews any empirical or inductive approach with his insistence that the collective Person is neither a psychophysical entity nor a factual social unit in the sense of any *particular* church, nation or society. Rather it is the 'experienced reality' (*erlebte Realität*) that makes possible the establishment of such particular units and communities. (FORM 512) Here, in a way that corresponds to his claim that while the essence of such values as the noble and the elegant first appear in our experience of men and things such values are not reducible to the objects and states in which they appear, Scheler would have us see that the collective Person lies behind any given collectivity. Moreover, the collective aspect of personality is, as it were, the *raison d'étre* of any and all particular or historical churches, nations and peoples.

As I read Scheler he is striving here to provide a transcendental account for the communal nature of humankind that will do justice to the crucial play of individual and collective concerns in any genuine community. By so doing he is able to acknowledge the existence of common ends that surpass the interests, and indeed, the existence of any member of the community. The collective Person, he notes, endures despite the death of any of its members. By the same token, in highlighting the personal quality of the collective, he can remain sensitive to the fact that communal values must be, in the final analysis, human or personal values. Thus, we may legitimately speak of the 'integrity', the 'honour', the 'corruptibility', or the 'debasement', of a church, a nation or a people. In this way we are led beneath the institutional form of such social units to speak meaningfully of their substantive qualities, qualities that Scheler will insist are ultimately personal and, thus, moral.

In a later work on *The Nature of Sympathy*, we come to appreciate just how full and profound this nexus of individuality, community and morality is.

> Taken by itself indeed, the moral consciousness offers a 'guarantee' that is not direct, let alone primary, but *indirect*, not only for the possibility of value, but also for the existence of other people. Nor does this apply to some one moral act or another, but to all morally relevant acts, experiences and states, in so far as they contain an intentional reference to other moral persons; obligation, merit, responsibility, consciousness of duty, love, promise-keeping, gratitude and so on, all refer, by the very nature of the acts themselves, to other people, without implying that such persons must already have been encountered in some sort of experience, and above all without warranting the assumption that these intrinsically social acts (as we shall call them), can only have occurred and originated in the actual commerce of men with one another. For on closer examination it appears, rather, that these acts and experiences are such that they cannot be reduced to a combination of more elementary acts and experiences of a *pre*-social kind, together with some sort of experience of other human beings. They demonstrate that even the *essential* character of human consciousness is such that the community is in some sense implicit in every individual, and that man is not only part of society, but that society and the social bond are an essential part of himself; that not only is the 'I' a member of the 'We' but also that the 'We' is a necessary member of the 'I'.[8]

This passage may help clarify why Scheler believes he can at one moment speak of the collective Person as an aspect of the finite or individual Person and, at another, characterise those entities we more typically understand as social or cultural institutions, that is, the nation and the church, as the embodiment or the expression of a collective personality. Any particular community, such as a church, is an expression of the essentially communal nature of humankind or, to adopt the approach with which we should now be familiar, this communal aspect of our nature is the *a priori*, universal, and necessary condition for the formation of any particular community.

The citation from the work on sympathy further indicates that Scheler never abandons his commitment to the cognitive and experiential primacy of *Wertnehmung*. (See the discussion of 'Scheler's Conception of Values' in chapter 3.) Indeed, unless he extends the primordial character of value-ception to encompass the social and communal dimension of human experience it is difficult to see how he can sustain the striking claim that the peculiarly social values – responsibility, love, and so on – reveal a sense of community which is so deep and intrinsic that it does not presuppose or assume any actual commerce with other men. And there can be no doubt that this is his intention. In the *Formalismus*, and in a later passage from the work on sympathy, he asserts that a Robinson Crusoe, who had never perceived any of his own kind, or any evidence for their existence, would still have a sense of community, even though this sense would only reveal itself in the consciousness of an emptiness or absence.[9] In other words, Crusoe would be lonely.

In my view, these observations on the sense of community are among Scheler's most telling insights. Whether we accede to all of his claims or not, he does help to give philosophical substance to our recognition, within the individual who is unable or unwilling to enter into association or communion with others, of an unrealised potentiality whose actualisation would contribute to a fuller, and thereby, more completely human life. In this sense, the unloving father, no less than the autistic child, is an instance of arrested development. What is more, with his characterisation of the various forms of community as collective Persons, Scheler captures the sense in which these are, indeed, not merely institutional arrangements of human association but, rather, moral entities. But, precisely how, and to what extent, this is the case is a matter that still needs to be clarified.

LIFE-COMMUNITY AND SOCIETY

Once we acknowledge that the sense of community is a unique and irreducible feature of experience, then Scheler's concept of the *Gesamtperson* is a consistent development in his ethics, one that is strictly analogous to his deduction of the Person as the necessary condition for all acts of goodness or evil. But, to this point, the discussion has revealed only one dimension of the collective Person, namely its role as the ground for the sense of community that is a precious capacity of all finite Persons.

However, Scheler is not content to rest with the elaboration of this relationship. Between the collective Person, understood as an essential element of any finite personality, and any particular social expression of our communal nature as church or nation, stands the 'life-community' (*Lebensgemeinschaft*). In this expression of community the *Gesamtperson* lives in solidarity with others to constitute such natural associations as the family and the tribe, wherein each member is mutually responsible for the intentions, the acts and the deeds of the whole community.

One distinctive feature of the life-community is that the values it expresses – those values which are manifest in habit (*Sitte*), custom (*Brauch*), cult, fashion (*Tracht*) and so on – is the tissue thin distinction Scheler draws between personal and communal values. While it is legitimate to speak of communal goals and intentions, and while the life-community can rightfully be seen as a natural living entity, Scheler finds it important to stress that the life-community is not a collective Person. This is because, Scheler insists, there is no collective will capable of choosing and bearing responsibility for the results of such choices. Only the *Gesamtperson*, understood as the unit of co-responsibility upon which the possibility of any life-community is fashioned and sustained, possesses the attribute of will. Thus, there is a crucial distinction to be preserved between the values of the life-community, which have the quality of thing-like values, and the values of the Person. (FORM 517)

In part, these observations reflect Scheler's persistent intention to affirm the non-objective character of the Person which mandates that the Person can never be treated as a thing. Yet, we have seen that he does feel justified in speaking of some forms of community as collective Persons. It would seem, then, that by insisting on the non-personal character of the life-community Scheler intends to suggest that such natural forms of human association as the family, the clan and the tribe do not presuppose the personal will, responsibility or initiative of their members. Here there is not, as there will be in society, any sense of individual responsibility. Rather, these are viable communities insofar as the will of each member is fused with others in a state of co-responsibility or solidarity. As members of life-communities we are, in effect, interchangeable parts of a common project bound together for the purpose of sustaining our common physical existence.

It is these natural and vital forms of human association, Scheler argues, that the philosophers of the eighteenth century mistakenly perceived as 'primitive' forms of society whose significance rested only with the extent to which they represented an important developmental stage in the social and political evolution of humankind. (FORM 527) Missing from this perspective is any recognition that life-communities are essential and *enduring* expressions of human solidarity that secure our collective physical existence while in turn, as we shall see in the discussion of social Persons, providing a moral content to liberal-democratic societies that no legal or contractarian arrangements can ensure.

It is clear that for Scheler life-communities occupy a position in his typology of social formations that roughly corresponds to the place of vital values in the hierarchy of values. Thus, their normative standing is less than those expressions of the collective Person – that is, nation and church – which are the social complement of spiritual values. Nonetheless, Scheler reminds us that the experience of solidarity in community is a vital and abiding expression of human nature. Moreover, his analysis of life-communities harbours an important principle for our time which, in ways reminiscent of Scheler's age, is marked by the rise of mass movements – white supremacy, religious fundamentalism and so on – that often appear to have a will of their own. By restricting the active and willful expressions of communal intentions to the domain of Persons in a state of co-responsibility, Scheler establishes a philosophical barrier against those forms of political and social action which claim to derive their legitimacy from a collective and anonymous 'we'. Here we are reminded that, at bottom, cults and peoples do not will and act. Rather, the movements we are often tempted to ascribe to such faceless entities represent the actions and reactions of concrete Persons expressing themselves in a collective manner; individuals, Scheler is insisting, who each bear co-responsibility for the life and deeds of their communities.

But as I have indicated, for Scheler, the common responsibility borne by members of any life-community occupies a position in the array of communal and social forms of human expression that is analogous to the place of vital values in the hierarchy of human goods. The mutual responsibility evident in any life-community is not one felt or known as responsibility *per se* because the life-community (family, tribe or clan) is an association governed by natural necessity. As Scheler puts it, the life-community comprises those who are 'not yet mature' (as well as domestic animals). (FORM 518)

This all inclusive characterisation of what comprises membership in life-communities signals the distinction Scheler would draw between such communities and society (*Gesellschaft*). While the unity of a life-community is a natural unity, the unity of society is established through such artificial means as contracts, constitutions, legislation, and so on. If the member of a life-community is responsible for the whole of the community (in the manner of mutual or co-responsibility), the prevailing principle of society is one of exclusive responsibility for self. In other words, in society the individual (*Einzelperson*) is not suspended or qualified by the *Gesamtperson*, as it is in the life-community; on the contrary, society exists for the sake of the individual. (FORM 517–519)

However, despite this important distinction between the life-community and society, the difference between them is not an exclusive one. On the contrary, Scheler insists that society presupposes community, 'the fundamental principle is: no society without community. . . All possible society is founded through community'. (FORM 520) At the heart of this assertion lies Scheler's disenchantment with the bloodless image of human relationships we encounter in the contractarian model of society. 'Just as boundless *trust* in one another is the basic attitude in community, boundless and primary *distrust* of all by all is the basic attitude in society.' (FORM 518)

But, Scheler suggests, distrust need not be the prevailing norm in society. Indeed, further reflection indicates that it *cannot* provide a coherent standard for any genuinely civil society. Unless contracts between individuals – which are the guiding motif of purely societal relationships – are enlivened by the prior experience of mutual or joint liability (*solidarische*) that is a basic feature of life-communities, the principle of duty upon which contracts ultimately rely is undermined. In other words, civic duty requires an attitude of 'moral faithfulness' that cannot be grounded in an appeal to some other contract, not even the 'social contract' itself. This process of infinite regress, whereby social contract theorists seek to ground any particular obligation in some prior obligation can never establish the binding character of obligation itself. Rather, the promissary element that lies within all contracts 'has its source in the *solidary* obligation of the members of the community to realise their dutiful commitments to the content (*Inhalte*) of the community. A so-called contract *without* this foundation would not be a contract, but merely a fiction'. (FORM 521)

Here Scheler's observations can be read as a response to a problem that every serious student of such political philosophers as Hobbes, Locke or Rawls must eventually confront, namely, the hypothetical character of the original social contract. Against the fiction of the contractarians' state of nature Scheler offers a more realistic portrait: one of a communal and cultural infrastructure within which commitments, duties and obligations are part of the daily course of human association. We are prepared, Scheler is arguing, for the artificial obligations and ties of civil society by and within the immediate and 'natural' bonds and expressions of community.

When this communal substance is recognised and comes to be an element in the web of legal and contractual social relationships we find '*the unity of independent, spiritual and individual single Persons "in" an independent, spiritual, individual collective Person*'. (FORM 522) As illustration Scheler cites the expression of social unity which has its historical discovery with the early Christian conception of a community founded on mutual love. There the existence and value of the individual and the collective are each affirmed and sustained. In this way Scheler would dissolve the political antinomy between liberalism and conservatism – between an account of society which adopts as its paradigm legally binding contracts between autonomous individuals and one which privileges the image of the people as a corporate polity – by making the latter an enduring and essential constituent of the former.

SOCIETY AS A MORAL ASSOCIATION

No respectable commentary on the preceding discussion can fail to note that the categories of social and communal existence Scheler develops are not altogether consistent with his depiction of the Person in his account of the value hierarchy. There he was careful to restrict any relationship between the Person and values to the realms of spiritual and holy values. It was not the Person as such but the indeterminate idea of a living-sensuous being that served as the *a priori* condition for the lower modality of vital values. Now we have been given a significantly expanded conception of the Person – and, concurrently, a much more precise designation of a living-sensuous being – with Scheler's characterisation of a finite Person capable of expressing itself as both an individual and a collective subject. This turn is in keeping with the tenor of Part Two in the *Formalismus* where, as we noted at the outset of this chapter, Scheler's reflections are far more didactic than those which marked his effort to appropriate the phenomenological method in his deduction of the material *a priori* content of normative experience.

However, despite the unacknowledged ambiguity which marks the conceptualisations of the Person that are elaborated in the two main sections of Scheler's treatise, a consideration of the relationship that obtains between his communal-social theory and the expanded conception of the Person which emerges at the core of this theory is well worth pursuing.

The main import of Scheler's remarks on the individual Person and the collective Person – each, we should emphasise, a manifestation of what lies within the capacity of each finite Person – and the theory of social units they suggest, is that there are certain values that cannot be realised without the suspension or overcoming of individuality. There can, in this account, be no familial love or brotherhood, no tribal culture or lore, and no communal fealty or purpose, without the capacity and willingness of the individual to surmount his or her private interests in favour of those which sustain the life-community. But, Scheler implies, there is no loss of personality in this move. The expression of communal values involves neither the sacrifice of the individual nor the loss of individuality. On the contrary, it entails an *expansion* of the self insofar as it bespeaks an *essential* facet of personality. Further, the individual is not lost in the realisation of communal values since it is the Person, now viewed as a member of a collective, who bears with every other member co-responsibility for the actualisation of communal values and thereby ensures their persistence. When Scheler observes that each *Gesamtperson* bears responsibility for the whole of the com-

munity he is enriching, rather than diminishing the role of the
Person and the individual. Thus, we can understand the sense of
irreplaceable loss that a family experiences with the death of one
of its members even as they know that life and the family will 'go
on'. So too, we can measure the extent to which the abdication of
responsibility or the desertion of one member is taken as a threat
by every other member of a closely knit tribe or community.

In this way Scheler's attempts to show how and where the
Person and the qualities we associate with personality might
remain at the core of any theory of community does much to
overcome the persistent dichotomy with which we often perceive, and falsely portray, the relationship between the individual
and the group. But, if we pursue the implications of his theory
of community and society there seems no compelling reason
to confine the unity of the individual and the collective to
the context of life-communities. If civil society simultaneously
presupposes and contains the experience of community, then it
would seem that many of the conditions which prevail between
the Person and community must also apply to that between the
Person and society. To expand upon one of Scheler's own illustrations, duty towards others in society rests upon the capacity
to enter into that relationship of mutual trust and endeavour that
is captured in the notion of solidarity. In this fashion, all genuine
societal contracts would presuppose this capacity. Thus, that
network of agreements, institutions and organisations that many
Marxists designate as the 'superstructure' of society – and many
liberals tend to view as the sum and substance of society – must
be predicated upon the implied allegiance of its members, even
though that allegiance is ostensibly certified by what Scheler
would consider artificial means: oaths, pledges and so on.

It is difficult to determine whether or not these last observations accurately reflect Scheler's intent. For, here again, his
discussion is ambiguous. At some points he appears to reject
the interpretation I am offering. He claims, for example, that
society exists to serve the interests individuals have in the lesser
values of the useful and the agreeable. And, insofar as these are
interests exclusive to particular individuals, they cannot serve
as the ground of social unity but are inherently divisive. (FORM
518–519) But this is an unjustifiably austere and instrumental
image of society that ignores the extent to which there are
values, which in Scheler's own terms comprise the highest

personal values, that can be realised only in and through society. To cite figures he would doubtless want to celebrate, the works of Michelangelo, Goethe and Hegel drew upon resources far more extensive than one would find in any simple, primitive or 'natural' community; such works were in significant measure coloured and sustained by the elaborate division of social and economic labour characteristic of civil societies. And if the artistic, literary and philosophic values which received their expression in the post-feudal era presupposed, in significant ways, the historical passage from medieval communities to civil societies, the same considerations apply even more vigorously to those values whose meaning and significance is ineluctably social, values such as 'freedom', 'universal justice', and 'equality', Thus, while it may be reasonable to contend, as Scheler does, that in the final analysis society serves as a means for the achievement of purposes and goals that are individual, it does not follow that these ends are narrowly utilitarian or inherently divisive.

As his account of the communal and social character of the Person moves to its conclusion Scheler's thought takes a turn which indicates that, indeed, he is aware that civil society occupies an essential place in the shaping and expression of morality. While he maintains his earlier position that only the concrete Person can be the 'bearer' of values, Scheler notes that there is a specific set of values – among them, 'reputation', 'dignity', and 'civil honour' – that can be expressed only within the context of society. (FORM 553) These are the values he attributes to the social Person (*soziale Person*), a subject he variously describes in terms of specific and individual functions, for example, those of the judge, and general social formations, for instance, the church and the nation. While his presentation here is among the most confounding and inconclusive in Part Two of the *Formalismus*, it does serve to demonstrate his awareness that the values attendant upon civil society entail more than the goods of the utilitarian, the useful and the agreeable.

In the final analysis we can only speculate as to whether or not further reflections on the nature of community and society would have led Scheler towards the full elaboration of a moral conception of civil society, one which, in effect, marries the legal structure of liberal rights and obligations to the corporate polity of classical conservatism. I have, of course, argued that it would be possible to do so without disrupting the basic structure of his philosophy. But it is quite clear that to do so would be to embark upon a thematic development at variance with Scheler's ultimate concern. For, as we shall see in chapter 6, it is not the communal and social aspects of moral experience that will be consummate in Scheler's ethics. Rather, all the distinctions he so laboriously draws will come to be subsumed in one paradigm expression of the Person, namely, the act of philosophical reflection.

6

The Primacy of Philosophical Experience

THE MORAL UPSURGE AND THE WHOLE MAN[1]

In the foregoing discussion we have traced Scheler's arguments for the primacy of value-cognition over all other forms of cognition and willing. And we have taken the measure of his insistence that in the material ethics of values it is the Person which serves as the ultimate moral concept. When Scheler turns his attention to 'The Nature of Philosophy' in his *On the Eternal in Man*, these two definitive themes are telescoped, with the result that philosophical knowledge becomes a feature of the moral bearing of the philosopher.

Just as he earlier moved from the study of values to a consideration of the Person as the active bearer of values, so Scheler now proceeds to ground his study of philosophy in a consideration of the act of philosophy itself. This he does, not simply out of an abiding interest in the various types of Person and expressions of personality (although that interest is clearly present), but out of a conviction that the best way to describe the nature of philosophy is to clarify the basic personal attitude of the philosopher.

> I am convinced that, heuristically at least. . . this method of determining a sphere of relevance by reference to the type of Person is both more certain and less equivocal in its results than any other procedure. How much easier it is for us to make up our minds whether a man is a true artist or true saint than to decide what art is and what religion! (EM 71)

This approach does not imply, however, that Scheler embarks upon this study with no preconceptions about the nature of philosophy. On the contrary, he commences with the premiss

109

that philosophy is an autonomous discipline, and as such can neither be reduced to the terms and concerns of other disciplines, nor (as we would expect) deduced from any empirical set of events and works. Indeed, it is this very autonomy that leads him to adopt the present course of inquiry.

> It is, for instance, quite unthinkable that we should want to find out by this method the realm of physics, zoology, and so on and so forth. The procedure is possible, meaningful and heuristically necessary only for those absolutely autonomous regions of being and value which may be defined neither through empirically determinable object-groups (*Gegenstandsreihen*) nor through any positive human need which arose *before* the attitude and its resultant activity, and demanded to be 'met'. In these cases entities and values form closed, self-contained, self-consistent realms. (EM 71)

Scheler's intention, then, is to locate the *idea*, as yet hidden from our judging, conceptual consciousness, of a certain universally human, pre-eminently intellectual *attitude* to things, an attitude of which we have, constituted as an objective *personality*, a mental image enabling us, without determining the attitude's positive *content*, to say whether an object conforms to or deviates from it. (EM 71)

Taking his initial clue from the ancients, Scheler observes that this attitude involves an element of love or 'the highest and purest form of what he (Plato) calls *eros*. . . the indwelling tendency of all imperfect being towards perfect being'. (EM 73) But, with philosophy 'perfect being' has a specific meaning, namely, essential reality or the unchanging being of beings (essences) through which everything contingent and relative exists. Thus, 'we may define the nature of the mental attitude which underlines all philosophical thinking as: *a love-determined movement of the inmost personal Self of a finite being towards participation in the essential reality of all possibles*. A man who takes up this attitude to the world belongs, in so far as he does take it up, to the essential type "philosopher" '. (EM 74)

With this, two explanatory observations seem called for. First, while Scheler presents this characterisation of philosophy and the philosopher with little preparatory argumentation, it certainly does not signify an unexpected development in his thought. We have seen throughout that his is, in large degree, a philosophy primarily concerned with essential, that is, absolute and unchanging states of being and, more specifically, we have noted that in his explication of the hierarchy of values he cites philosophical truth as one instance of a non-contingent (which is to say, 'absolute') value. Second, Scheler is quick to point out that this first definition gives only a general description of the philosophical act whose implications he subsequently attempts to flesh out.

As a first qualification Scheler notes that the participation of the philosopher in reality must be cognitive. Without denying, indeed, by eloquently affirming other forms of essential wisdom he insists that the wisdom peculiar to philosophy must take the form of knowledge. Hence, if the experience of the 'primal essence' involved 'dreaming the Brahma's dreams' or 'in Buddha's sense. . . the "entry into Nirvana",' the philosopher would still not be participating in Reality *qua* philosopher. (EM 75) Only after he had reflected upon his journey and its significance could he claim to have achieved philosophical participation. And, 'anyone. . . who would like to escape this *formal* "intellectualism" of philosophy does not know what he is asking. One can only say to him that he has mistaken his vocation, but that he has no right to make out philosophy and the philosopher to be other than they are'. (EM 75)[2]

A second feature of the philosophical act rests with its wholistic character. Again citing Plato, Scheler notes that 'in philosophy the whole man, not only his isolated intellect or isolated sensibility, etc., should seek participation in Reality'. (EM 90) Whereas the sciences

> demand the exercise of quite distinct *partial* functions of the human mind; one, for example, will require more skill in reasoning or observation, another greater ability to draw conclusions or make inductive discoveries. . . from the outset the *concrete whole* of the human mind engages in philosophical thinking, and that in a sense which I would describe as 'bracing and embracing' (*überspannend*) whatever particular group of functions is active at a given time. (EM 90)

It is at this stage of his discussion that Scheler makes his most ambitious claim for philosophy and the philosophical act. Because of its wholism philosophy stands above, not only the sciences, but art and religion as well. Only the philosopher 're:ntegrates, in his innermost self, the intrinsically disintegrated forms of insights and mental orientation which are accepted in the sciences, arts, or religion as separate and distinct, related as they are to the specific conditions and possibilities of whatever regions of values and being are relevant to a given branch of knowledge'. (EM 90)

When this statement is considered in the context of his previous claims, it would seem to indicate Scheler's attempt to achieve a synthesis of the many categories and concepts that emerge in his previous analyses. If, for example, the whole Man – intellect and sensibility – seeks participation in reality, then the basic dichotomy within the value hierarchy, between vital and spiritual values, is abrogated in the philosophical act. Similarly, if this act reintegrates the values and ontological distinctions which separate art, science and religion, then the discrepancy between the various modes and levels of spiritual values is annulled.

The expectation that we have at last reached the long awaited, and often promised, synthesis of Scheler's various normative concerns is strengthened by his description of the philosophical act as a moral upsurge (*ein moralischer Aufschwung*). The term expresses a continuity with his reflections on ethics and, taken together with his insistence that this is an act involving the whole Man (*des ganzen Menschen*), signals a move which will appropriate all other values and experiences of values. But, his further elaboration of this movement reveals that such is not to be the case and that, regrettably, Scheler has something far less comprehensive in mind.

In its manifestation as a moral upsurge, the philosophical act entails the suspension of all historical and empirical world views, which Scheler describes with the inclusive phrase, natural *Weltanschauung*. 'A primary feature of the natural *Weltanschauung* is that the subject takes the environmental world of the moment, or all possible environmental worlds to be *the* world-being (*Weltsein*)' (EM 93) But, 'philosophical cognition is aimed into an entirely *different* sphere of being, which lies outside and beyond any mere environment'. (EM 94) Further, in a remark which clearly recalls and invokes the basic dualism within the hierarchy of values, Scheler claims that this cognitive act necessarily entails a break with that outlook in which 'the mind's only possible objects must be ontically relative to life, relative to the "vital" in general, hence *also* – of necessity – relative to some specific corporeal, instinctual, sensory system'. (EM 94–95)

Unlike Scheler's discussion of the various expressions of personality in the *Formalismus*, the presentation here insists that the moral upsurge does indeed carry with it the need to deny the claims and values of the lived world, and by implication, the life-community.

> Within this combination of basic moral acts conducive to philosophical cognition we discern one of positive and two of negative character; they must work together in unitary interaction if a man is to reach the threshold of knowing the object of philosophy:
>
> 1. *the whole spiritual Person must love absolute value and being;*
> 2. *the natural self and ego must be humbled;*
> 3. *self-mastery must be achieved*: in this way it is possible to objectify the instinctual impulses of life, which are 'given' and experienced as 'of the flesh' and which must needs exert a constant influence in natural sensory perception. (EM 95)

This concatenation of moral acts reveals, as starkly as any other passage in Scheler's works, the extent to which the roots of his philosophy remain embedded in Kantian soil. Nowhere does Kant express with more vigour the principle that the repression of all 'pathological' considerations is a necessary prerequisite of morality. A brief summary of the major steps Scheler has taken in these reflections on the nature and place of philosophy suffices to indicate that this is, indeed, the conclusion to which he is driven. He has, in his exposition of the value hierarchy situated philosophical truth within the realm of spiritual values. Subsequently, we saw that it is the Person as act-centre that is the bearer of all specifically moral values. And, finally, we discover that the most consummate act of the Person – consummate in so far as it surveys and embraces all other spiritual values, is the act of philosophical cognition.

Thus, with his characterisation of the moral upsurge Scheler does achieve some measure of a synthesis of many of the themes he develops along the way: the notion of spiritual values, the various expressions of the Person, and morality as the property of an act, rather than of a substantive or objective state of reality. But, this is a synthesis which excludes the whole realm of vital values and, as such, falls short of his initial intention to deal with the fullness of our value experience in a manner that would flesh out Kant's 'colossus of steel and bronze'. In the remainder of this chapter we shall see that, despite a final attempt to deal with the notion of the whole or 'total' man, Scheler remains firmly committed to a one-dimensional idealism.

THE OBJECT OF PHILOSOPHY

Before concluding his essay on the nature of philosophy Scheler deals more specifically with the character of that reality with which the philosopher seeks participation. This he does by elaborating upon three self-evident insights that, as he maintains, present themselves once the philosophical attitude or moral upsurge has been accomplished. The first such insight is expressed in the judgement which privileges being over non-being.

> The situation that *there is not nothing* is at one and the same time the object of the first and most direct self-evident insight and the object of the most intense, the ultimate philosophical *wonder*, though I grant that the emotional response cannot come to fruition until it has been preceded, among the emotional acts conducive to the philosophical attitude, by the adoption of that humility which abolishes the taken-for-granted, self-evident character of being as a fundamental fact and even undermines it as an *obvious* fact. (EM 98–99)

At first reading this claim appears ambiguous: Scheler speaks of the self-evident character of being and the self-evident insight that there is not nothing. The ambiguity is absolved, however, once we recall the setting of the moral upsurge. The character of being is self-evident and non-problematic only for those who adopt the perspective of the natural *Weltanschauung*. But when the philosopher breaks with that perspective and in the process adopts an attitude of humility, then the nature and primacy of being is thrown into question. For in the act of humbling himself there is a moment when the philosopher entertains the possibility of nothingness, when he realises, in other words, the relativity of his own existence. Thus, 'whoever has not, so to speak, looked into the *abyss of absolute nothingness* will indeed completely overlook the eminent positivity inherent in the insight that there is something, and not nothing. . .' (EM 99)

This recognition of his own contingent existence issues in the second insight, namely, that in so far as all relative or non-absolute entities exist, they do so by virtue of their relationship to absolute being.

> For if . . . there is something rather than nothing, then in our own 'examples' to be reviewed at will that part of them which is relative not-being . . . can indeed be attributed to the possible contingencies and relativities which their being possesses from other entities (*von anderen sein besistz*) . . .but this is never possible in respect of their positive being itself . . .To anyone who denies this proposition one can only show that the mere *attempt* of denial and all his arguments presuppose that even in his own intention the absolute is in fact *given* to him. . .Looking through the web of any relative entity. . . he looks *through,* but in the direction of the absolute entity. (EM 100–101)

Scheler acknowledges that there are logical difficulties with this second purported insight (while he does not specify what they are we might question, for one, the implied relationship of unilateral dependency between absolute being and those lesser degrees of being we recognise in relative states of existence) but he skirts them with the now familiar appeal to intuition. However, what is significant for our study is not the internal consistency of his argument, but the fact that it provides a further instance of the turn in his philosophy away from the concrete and towards a highly speculative metaphysics. The trend continues as he takes up the relationship between essence and existence.

The third self-evident insight is expressed in the judgement that 'every possible entity must necessarily possess a qualitative *quid-est*, an essence and also an *existentia*'. (EM 102) As Scheler elaborates upon this principle it becomes apparent that it expresses a function of the dualism between relative and absolute being that has come to assume a dominant position in his thought. For, while he insists that any given entity possesses both existence and essence there is, in his judgement, an exclusive difference between the two states of being. Knowledge of essences is,

> entirely different from existential knowledge . . .Once we have fully perceived the pure essential content of an object (or an act), or a particular arrangement or interrelation of such essences, our knowledge has peculiarities which fundamentally distinguish it from all knowledge of the realm of relative and contingent existence. It is *definitive*, thus capable of increase or diminution – that is to say, it is strictly *self-evident*, whereas knowledge of contingency, however attained . . . never arrives at more than presumptive truth, certainly conditional on the findings of a later experience or an adjustment to a more conclusive context. (EM 102–103)

At this point it is important to bear in mind that, for Scheler, philosophical knowledge expresses an attempt by the philosopher to participate in reality. Hence, the distinction he is marking between knowledge of existence and knowledge of essence has a range of significance that surpasses the merely epistemological. In the first place, this distinction, together with that which he draws between relative and absolute being, clearly points to an ontological rupture between the realm of existence and the realm of essence.[3] The one attempt he makes to heal this rupture only serves to confirm it. Scheler notes that in the case of the absolute entity there is no true dichotomy, that here essence and existence are fused in one, but then – in apparent deference to the third purported self-evident insight – he immediately observes that, in this instance as well, we must hypothetically envisage a dichotomy within which essence takes primacy over existence.[4]

The second indication that we are dealing here with claims whose significance is ontological comes with the recognition that it is an essential realm of being Scheler has in mind when he speaks of reality. This has been implicit from the moment he posits the need for a break with the natural *Weltanschauung* as a necessary condition for the philosophical act. But, now that the precise character of 'reality' has been defined, we can see the full import of Scheler's position. If the philosophical act is ultimately defined as an attempt to achieve participation by the whole man with a mode of being that is both essential and absolute, then the philosopher, in so far as he is an existential and contingent being, has set himself an impossible task. Like Kant before him, Scheler is forced to the conclusion that only as a rational being can Man rise above the level of contingency and that it is this *rational* capacity that is the hallmark of his morality.[5]

My continued emphasis on the dualisms and dichotomies which pervade Scheler's thought – between sensibility and intellect, life and spirit, relative and absolute states of being – would be contentious and, in large measure, unwarranted were it not for the fact that he remains oblivious to their implications, if not of their presence. For example, within the context of the present discussion he explicitly takes issue with Plato's view that philosophical activity involves a conflict between the senses and the intellect. Scheler further renounces what he interprets as Plato's asceticism and the notion that the life of the philosopher may be characterised as a *'dying to all eternity'*. (EM 73) And yet, we have seen that these images and descriptions are wholly appropriate to the philosophical act as Scheler himself describes it.

There is yet another reason for dwelling on this issue. It does not, as might be suspected, occupy an isolated or fleeting moment in Scheler's philosophy but, quite the contrary, is one of that philosophy's most abiding, albeit problematic, themes. Thus, despite the fact that many of Scheler's philosophic interests and positions shifted over the years, we find in his last works that the dichotomy between the realm of the intellect and the realm of the senses has become a firmly entrenched feature of his thought.

THE IDEAL OF THE TOTAL MAN

A few months before his unexpected death Scheler addressed the *Deutsche Hochschule für Politik* on the subject, *Der Mensch im Weltalter des Ausgleiches* (Man in an Era of Adjustment).[6] In his remarks he again considered the task of overcoming the 'opposition between power and spirit', and called upon his audience to contemplate a rebirth of leadership in Germany that would unify the vital and spiritual resources of that nation within the context of a parliamentary democracy, specifically the Weimar Republic. (PP 94)

Given Scheler's demonstrated concern with personal types it is not surprising that his call would take the form of a demand to develop a type of leader, an 'élite' type, who would be capable of unifying all the divisions and contrasts that, in Scheler's view, must express themselves through the democratic process. What is somewhat surprising, and given the political aftermath of the Weimar Republic, salutary, is the extent to which he was insistent that this new type of leader must break with time-honoured patterns and processes. The new élite must most explicitly,

> *not* be an élite of mere blood and tradition like the old Prussian aristocracy and the caste of state employees which it sponsored. The tasks of our epoch call for human qualities and abilities unlikely to be transmitted from father to son by the principles of psychic inheritance. Nor will the élite rise from one of the all too numerous parties which have such strong ideological orientations. (PP 95)

Here Scheler recognised that the depth of the opposition between the forces of life and the forces of spirit – in society, no less than in the individual – together with the epochal nature of the times, conspired so decisively to reinforce one another that the unity he sought could only be achieved through a '*transformation of man himself*', of the nature of his internal constitution in body, mind, and spirit'. (PP 97)

But is such a transformation possible? As we explore his answer we will find it haunted by a deep seated ambiguity that reveals the extent to which, despite his recognition of the necessity to pass beyond the persona of the old Adam towards the creation of an integrated personality, he is unable to achieve for himself a total liberation from his own (philosophical) past.

> Speaking of the future and of a new image of man, I cannot conceive any future image which envisages an automatic transformation, whether positive or negative, of man's organic nature, natural aptitude, but only one which represents an 'ideal' that admits man's *freedom to develop himself*, an ideal implying that man himself will shape that infinitely plastic segment of his nature which can be influenced directly or indirectly by spirit and will. What comes from the spirit does not come automatically, not does it come of itself. It must be guided! In this sense we accept the word of the Frenchman Gratry: 'Not only the individual, but also humanity can end as saint or criminal, depending on how it directs its *will*.' Man is

a creature whose very essence is the open decision. What does he want to *be* and to *become*?

However, this ideal for man is, if it must have a name, the '*total man*', not the 'superman' conceived separately from the masses and from all democracy. Through the ideal of the total man, superman and subman are to become *human*. (PP 101)

There can be no denying that, taken in its entirety, this declaration resounds with optimism, perhaps reflective of the euphoria which gripped Germany and the West prior to the economic and political disaster of the 1930s. But, its promise that the very essence of Man is an 'open decision' seems to be betrayed by his admission of the limiting conditions present in 'man's organic, natural aptitude'.

At one point in his remarks Scheler is absolutely uncompromising in his acknowledgement of these conditions: 'we must completely abandon all thought of an essential transformation of man in the *biological*, especially in the morphological sense'. (PP 98) Here it seems that he is prepared to settle for a limited transformation that will touch only those dimensions of human nature that are, as 'plastic', somehow distinct from the organic. But, as we shall see, the structure of his philosophical anthropology forces him to entertain and, ultimately, propose a transformation that does, indeed, go to the heart of Man's organic and biological existence.

To understand why this is so we must recall the image of man that emerged in Scheler's earlier reflections on the hierarchy of values. There we found that the entire sphere of vital values encompasses phenomena that are, in the largest sense, biological – the values which pertain to Man as a sensuous Being: pleasure, pain, and the value of life together with its attendant values of health, disease and so on. Now, in my reading of this text, the earlier commitment to the depiction of vital values as essential (but not, in any sense, the highest) constituents of human nature drives Scheler beyond the premise that the transformation of human nature is limited by biological conditions, to employ the prospect of their alteration as a transient, although *necessary*, step towards the fulfillment of the ideal of the total man.

Within the context of the essay on 'Man in an Era of Adjustment' the familiar distinctions between sensibility and intellect, vital values and spiritual values are characterised in terms of the distinction between Dionysius and Apollo. Since, Scheler argues, the idea of total man is 'the idea of a man who contains and has realised *all* his essential capabilities', a minimal condition for its fulfillment will be an adjustment between the ideas of the Apollonian and the Dionysian man. (PP 102) In Scheler's view, and he cites considerable evidence in its support, Western civilisation has been characterised throughout its evolution by the sublimation of the Dionysian (the philosophy of life) by the Apollonian (the philosophy of ideas). The most obvious manifestation of this sublimation has been the persistence of an ascetic and excessive rationalism in Occidental culture.

> Ever since late antiquity and the appearance of Jesus, ever since the Judaic theistic view began to rule the Occident, the ascetic ideal has developed into a most *one-sided* species of man, in ever renewed forms and with completely different causal explanations. Finally, this species began seriously to endanger the equilibrium of human powers. First came the early Christian and patristic asceticism as an antithesis to the paganism of antiquity; then the asceticism of medieval monks and monasteries, relatively harmless since it affected only a small minority; then the progress of this ascetic ideal among the masses and 'laymen', not the least of all through Protestant asceticism, the 'advocates of the inner world', as Max Weber and Ernst Troeltsch called them; and finally and increasingly, the tremendous capitalistic 'asceticism of the golden idol' (Karl Marx), the asceticism of work and industry aiming for unlimited accumulation of products. (PP 108–109)

What is needed, Scheler argues, is a reversal of these priorities through a process of re-sublimation; 'the spiritually conscious act of reducing the amount of accumulated energy which the organism transfers to the brain or to the intellect, the apparent locus of all purely spiritual activity, that is, of all acts of ideation'. (PP 106–107) Remarkably, Scheler goes on to claim that this need is being answered. In a passage that is notable for its contemporary relevance, Scheler cites the anti-intellectualism and panvitalism which have come to characterise mass movements in Europe and America, the 'erotic customs of youth in all countries', modern psychoanalysis and the psychology of drives, the decreasing appreciation of the scholar and intellectual artist in favour of 'the "heroic types" in contemporary sport and cinema', and the 'feverish desire for "strength", "beauty", and " youth" ' as merely a few symptoms of

> a systematic revolt of man's drives in the new era against one sided sub-limation, against the exaggerated intellectualism of our fathers, their century-old ascetic practices, and their techniques of sublimation (already subconscious) which, up to the present, have fashioned Occidental man. For the time being, the gods of so called 'life' seem to have replaced the rule of the gods of the 'spirit'; for I do not consider this movement as a very transitory 'post-war phenomenon.' It has begun before the war, as the figure of Nietzsche suffices to show; he gave the word 'life' its magic sound. In fact, I see a collective movement, deeply rooted in the history of the Occident, aiming at a *redistribution* of man's *total energy* between the cortex and the rest of his organism. (PP 107–108)

This passage stands as one of the most radical of Scheler's pronouncements. For here he seeks to move to the very roots of the crisis in consciousness which appeared to many of his age, and, indeed, appears to many in our own time, as *the* affliction of the twentieth century. He indicates that in the social and cultural phenomena he cites, we are witnessing nothing less than a perversion of human nature, a perversion so consequential as to have engendered a reaction which is not merely sociological or cultural, but *organic*. Incredibly, however, Scheler seems oblivious to the radical character of his analysis and to the fact that, if his appraisal is correct, it belies his contention that we cannot conceive of any transformation in man's organic and natural aptitude. Only if we take his initial assertions with respect to the fixed biological character of Man in the narrowest sense, as though he intends to limit his observation to the context of a morphological shell within which dramatic physiological changes occur, can we square these latest claims with the contrast he initially drew between the 'organic, natural aptitude' and the 'plastic segments of human nature'. But, surely, a biological account of human nature must go beyond more than a mere depiction of the human form, to encompass such bio-chemical phenomena as Scheler's account of a possible redistribution of energy within the human organism.

Since Scheler never acknowledges the apparent inconsistency in his account of the nature and degree of any possible transformation of human nature, it is impossible to offer a definitive account of why he does not recognise that the redistribution of energy between the cortex and the rest of the human organism could signal that change in Man's natural aptitude that he has categorically removed from the realm of possibility. But one thing seems clear: admission of such a possibility would involve overturning or, at the very least, denying that many of the commitments established in his ethics have any historical or practical significance whatever. If, for example, the possible ascendence of the Dionysian (vital values) over the Apollonian (spiritual values) represents either an irreversible or a permanent transformation in Man's historical evolution as a species, then the absolute and *a priori* character of the value hierarchy becomes merely a momentary datum of philosophical reflection. But, clearly, Scheler's elaboration of this hierarchy intended more. The hierarchy of values was not simply a set of formal ideas, but the constant and unchanging material of human preferences, choices and intentions.

Thus, in order for Scheler to remain consistent with his earlier positions he must claim that the process of re-sublimation he is describing here signifies only a *modification* of the value hierarchy, a modification of the sort we considered in the discussion of 'Vorziehen' as Evidence for a Hierarchy of Values' in chapter 4. And this is not all. Unless he is to abandon or ignore that earlier work he must, after paying such heavy tribute to the importance of vital values, reaffirm their relative character and the related supremacy of spiritual values. With great subtlety, Scheler now moves to accomplish that end and restore the credibility of his earlier position.

The present ascendency of the Dionysian is, Scheler tells his audience, a healthy development and, when considered against the historical backdrop of the ascetic rationalism against which it is a clear reaction, one that might well last a century without accomplishing great harm. But, ultimately, it *is* reactionary, a 'counter-ideal', and, as such, is merely a first tentative step towards the realisation of the total man. (Scheler compares what he sees as the Dionysian excesses of the present era to the yearning for childhood found in the aged. The implication of the analogy is obvious: our age is old and tired, yet what is needed is not a 'second childhood', but a genuine rebirth that will issue in the new and 'total' Man.) The total man, then, will be one who has transcended this moment in history and appropriated the vital values, or the Dionysian principle, in a unity that embraces both the vital and the spiritual.

> The man who is most deeply rooted in the darkness of earth and nature, and of the *'natura naturans'* which produces all natural phenomena, *'natura naturata'*, the man who *simultaneously*, as a spiritual person, in his consciousness of self, reaches the utmost heights of the luminous world of ideas, that man is approaching the idea of total man, and, therewith, the idea of the substance of the very source of the world, through a constantly *growing interpenetration of spirit and drive.* (PP 111)

Once again, we find Scheler struggling to articulate a concept of Man that will unify the full panorama of human expression. And, once again, we find that unity dissolving almost as soon as it is spoken. Even with the above formulation there is the suggestion that all will not be harmonious between the vital and the spiritual, that instead, the natural drives and forces in Man will be subordinated as the Person moves to 'reach the utmost heights' of the intellectual world. This implication becomes clearer yet when Scheler describes the form that the appropriation of the natural, the Dionysian, and the vital will take. In contrast to the traditional approach which seeks 'to annul every pain and evil . . . from *without*, by transforming external irritations that cause it', he calls upon Western man to develop a *'systematic technique for overcoming suffering from within'.* (PP 113) This technique will express itself in 'an art of meditation, introspection, endurance, and contemplation of being', through which man will win *inner* power over the whole inferior, nonspiritual, psychophysical "life" '. (PP 114)

Therefore, for Scheler, nature and the values of life retain their relative and subordinate position, the supreme character of spiritual values – with the philosophical attitude primary among them – is reaffirmed. The total man (or woman) is, finally, not the subject who gives expression to all of his (or her) essential capabilities but, on the contrary, the one who endures by controlling the vital in the service of the spiritual.

Here we have the ultimate paradox and irony of Scheler's philosophical anthropology. His conception of the total man concludes in a new asceticism! In dialectical fashion, his thought has moved to posit the vitalism of our era as the long-awaited and necessary negation of the extreme spiritual intellectualism that has been definitive of Occidental culture. But this negation is to be short-lived, it represents only a transient moment that will ultimately be appropriated in, and submerged by, a new spiritualism that is made more complete by its sublimation of vital values and claims.

Thus, whether Scheler considers the values of life and sensibility within the context of a fixed and *a priori* hierarchy of values, or against the background of an unfolding process of human consciousness in time, the result is the same: these values are relative, inferior and contingent in their relation to the spiritual and intellectual goods. In this manner, the disjunction between thought and sensibility that was the point of departure for his Kant-critique persists throughout Scheler's philosophical development, to be preserved in his final reflections on human nature. What is more, Scheler's model of the end of human development, namely the 'total man' appears to be one which only the philosopher might approximate, just as we were led to wonder earlier whether, for Kant, any save the moral philosopher might qualify as an ethical subject.

In the next and concluding chapter of this study, we will explore the implications of this development for any attempt, such as Scheler's, to deal fully and adequately with all the features of our value experience. There, I will try to suggest an approach that might make it possible to overcome the dualisms that have continually compromised Scheler's attempt to present an integrated and wholistic image of Man.

7

Towards a Radical Humanism

When we assess Scheler's ethic in light of its expressed purpose to surpass Kant we must conclude that the effort is only a qualified success. What it accomplishes is much more akin to one of those modifications of Kant's ethic, to which Scheler refers in the first preface to the *Formalismus*, than it is to the intended breakthrough towards an ethic that is universal (insofar as it would articulate *a priori* categories and concepts) and objective (insofar as it would establish a transcendental foundation for the sensible content of our experience of values). In support of his appraisal I would cite three crucial areas in which Scheler is unable significantly to transcend Kant.

SCHELER'S IDEALISM

Perhaps the most crucial point on which Scheler's ambition miscarries is in his inability to overcome the dichotomy between thought and sensibility that he correctly analysed as the source of Kant's reluctance to assign sensibility a decisive role in moral judgements. The first indication that Scheler was falling short of his mark appeared in what I have termed his 'materialist reduction'. In seeking to break down the distinction between the formal and the material constituents in the experience of values by raising the material of that experience to *a priori* status, Scheler achieved a compromise between his position and Kant's that left the basic dualism between thought and sensibility intact. What Kant considers the purely formal elements of morality, such as the moral will, in Scheler's formulation becomes material for the will. Conversely, the experience of values, which Kant understands as too intimately related to sensibility to be of any aid in the establishment of a universal ethic, becomes for Scheler

125

a field in which one can intuit those universal and necessary relationships and concepts that, for Kant, can only be formal. The significant issue here is that Scheler and Kant are one in their contention that in order to grant such relationships and concepts the status of *a prioris* they must ultimately be freed of any empirical considerations.

In effect, what Scheler does is to move *through* and *beyond* a consideration of value-ception (*Wertnehmung*) to locate and articulate what he conceptualises as its essential features, features which both 'justify' and ground the experience or perception of values. As we have seen, this move parallels Kant's procedure in the *First Critique* that led him from the consideration of sense perception to the articulation of those transcendental conditions that render sense perception and, indeed, knowledge itself, possible. In neither case does the philosopher remain within the bounds of that experience that served as their point of departure. Both Kant and Scheler enter into a consideration of a transcendental realm itself, implicitly claiming that unless some break with the sensible world is achieved the universal and necessary character of their ethical principles will be compromised. In this way the distinction between the essential and the 'real' in Scheler (see the discussion of 'An Appraisal of the Hierarchy' in chapter 4) is a reflection and function of the distinction between thought and sensibility in Kant.

One of the more important implications of Scheler's adherence to a dualism between thought and sensibility is apparent in the second area where he does not manage wholly to surpass Kant, namely, in the doctrine of the Person. For both men the concept of the Person denotes Man's moral capacity and, more important, for both it is a concept established by means of a transcendental deduction. This latter feature has the effect of placing the Person beyond the realm of our individual and collective experiences and squarely within the framework of a transcendental idealism.

In our treatment of Kant we were able to trace the results of such an idealism without too much difficulty and eventually determine that, for him, the Person describes a potential and final end for humans which, by virtue of our sensuous nature, we can never fully attain. (See the discussion of 'Morality as Final Cause' in chapter 2.) But it is not until Scheler introduces the act of philosophising, and characterises it as the highest expression of the Person, that we see that in his case as well as that of Kant any consummate expression of the Person must elude us. There we learn that, as an attempt by the whole man to participate in an essential Reality which is, by definition, free of all existential determinations, the philosophical act is unattainable by any mortal being.

Scheler's attempt to make the philosophical act the highest expression of the Person points to the third area in which he remains firmly within the Kantian milieu. For Kant morality is a function of rationality because, in my judgement, Kant recognises an affinity between the capacity of Reason to impose universal criteria upon the various elements of experience and his own intention to develop ethical categories that would be universally applicable. Similarly, in his presentation of 'The Nature of Philosophy' Scheler takes care to stress the wholistic and inclusive character of rationality. It is not surprising, then, that as he seeks to articulate those values which are absolute and universal his ethics becomes increasingly idealistic with the philosophical spirit gaining ascendancy over the religious. Thus, although Scheler pursues a different course and is motivated by different considerations he ultimately establishes, as does Kant, an essential link between reason and morality.

All these features conspire to transform Scheler's attempt to address the material content of morality into a variety of idealism. With this characterisation I have in mind 'idealism' in both its descriptive and normative meanings. Scheler's ethics is ideal, first, to the degree that it assigns ontological and epistemological priority to the ideational elements of experience over its empirical – that is, its spatio-temporal – content. Even though these ideas are described as present in intuition, rather than discovered through the more familiar processes of reason (that is, deduction and induction) and even though they are often the ideas *of* matter (that is, the essential states of being that stand behind the variety of sensible experiences) they enjoy the same primacy and independence *vis-à-vis* the lived world of practical experience and activity that is characteristic of every philosophical idealism since Plato.

The normative dimension of Scheler's idealism is most evident in those passages which insist that neither the concept of the Person nor the notion of the 'total man' describes Man as he is.

Total man, in the absolute sense, is hardly close to us. It is the idea of a man who contains and has realized *all* his essential capacities. Indeed, he is as far from us as God who, in so far as we grasp his essence in spirit and life, is nothing but the *essentia* (essence) of man, only in infinite form and fullness. However, every age of human history knows *a relatively total man*, a *maximum* of total humanity which is accessible to it, a relative maximum of participation in the highest forms of human existence. (PP 102)

The purpose here is to construct, after a detailed consideration of human experience and activity, an ideal that will express the unique and fundamental features of human nature in the purest and highest form conceivable (hence the reference to God) and which will serve as a model for practice and a standard against which we might measure the progress or regress of any particular era, society or generation.

In these respects Scheler is, for all his attempts to appropriate the phenomenological method in the service of essential knowledge and truth, in the company of the great idealists and metaphysicians of the Western philosophical tradition: Plato, Thomas Aquinas, Descartes, Kant and so on. With them, Scheler's intention to transcend our daily, historical and collective experience of values in order to fund and redeem this experience threatens to leave us with a depiction of morality and the good so ethereal and so removed that our attempts to live and act as moral subjects appear, in contrast to the vision of the philosopher, mundane and incomplete.

Nonetheless, this judgement of Scheler's ethical studies need not, and should not, represent our final assessment of their merits. If we follow the lead of such contemporary scholars as Alasdair MacIntyre and Jürgen Habermas there is much to be gained from what Habermas would term an 'immanent critique' of Scheler and what MacIntyre might describe as a 'moral project' or 'moral discourse'.[1] From both perspectives, albeit for quite different reasons, we are invited to think beyond the logical flaws and ideological pretences that inevitably mark any attempt to ground the study of ethics in a comprehensive philosophical system and, by so doing, to rescue those themes, observations and claims that can give meaningful shape to our own moral understandings and experiences.

In any study of Scheler's work such a sympathetic reading as I am calling for is warranted by at least one motif in his thought that serves to distance him from many of the premises and problems that mark the systems of those traditional figures who were his philosophical forebears. This would be his persistent intention to honour and treat the full range of human expression – the negative as well as the positive expression of values, the nuances of personality that sustain and are in their turn nourished by life in differing forms of human association, and the immediate judgements of value that colour all subsequent perceptions of a situation or phenomenon – in a manner that will preserve the integrity and value of each such expression. To be sure, it is this concern that provokes many of the difficulties we encountered in this work, most notably, perhaps, the proliferation of distinctions, concepts and categories that often threaten to swamp the entire enterprise. What is more, as I have felt it necessary to stress in this concluding assessment, Scheler's rich depiction of our normative and moral experience is severely qualified by his insistence upon a transcendental foundation and locus for that experience. Ultimately, however, it is this dimension of his thought that can reward a careful study of his ethics.

While it is exceedingly difficult and problematic to establish unwavering philosophical foundations for our experience of personal dignity and the variety of moral expressions that flow from it, there are compelling pragmatic reasons for evaluating and prizing such experience. The concept of the Person, and the varieties of expressions Scheler assigns to it, can give critical substance to our understanding of the individual, historical and social development of humankind. If we were to relinquish or deny the capacity to identify, articulate and respond to the moral character of others, or to assess communal and social relationships in terms such as those Scheler provides, the language of morality would become even more dissonant than it now is. Surely, Scheler, no more than Kant, provides us with the secure and unshakeable foundation for ethics towards which they so laboriously strived. But, there is here *an* ethics that can contribute to the overcoming of the normative and value illiteracy that all of us who are involved in the teaching of ethics increasingly confront in our students. In this spirit, some concluding thoughts on the positive accomplishments and implications of Scheler's work may be appropriate.

SCHELER'S HUMANISM

At the outset of this chapter I suggested that while Scheler fell short of his stated intent to surpass the Kantian ethic, the turn towards a material ethics of values does represent a modification of Kant's ethic. Taken in itself, rather than in its relationship to the problems which inevitably confront any transcendental idealism, this modification represents a significant development in the history of ethical studies. Rather than limiting the consideration of our moral capacity to any single principle, such as the autonomy of the will, Scheler recognises that this capacity takes shape in a variety of expressions (loving, creating, willing and thinking) and becomes manifest in several settings (community, art, religion and philosophy). In this way Scheler 'humanises' ethics by tracing the imprint of our morality in the full panoply of works and gestures from which humankind is constituted.

The vehicle through which Scheler achieves this rich and expanded understanding of morality is, of course, his concept of the Person. He invites us to consider the Person as both the bearer of morality and the centre for *all* acts. Thus, our morality is brought to bear (either explicitly or implicitly) in the full range of human practices. From this perspective the labourer or farmer whose activities serve to sustain the values of life is not merely performing an instrumental or utilitarian task. Whatever instrumental value might accrue to their activities is, at bottom, a feature of the moral worth of life itself. Similarly, the primitive community, no less than advanced society, bears the stamp of human personality and, accordingly, must be recognised as a moral form of association.

We encountered a first, embryonic, expression of this theme in Scheler's contention that our most primordial relationship with the world is pervaded by perceptions and judgements of value. But this, in and of itself, does not give us the moral tenor of such values. This only emerged with Scheler's explication of the Person. If all our acts and deeds are fundamentally valuational, and if good and evil are properties invoked in every act of valuation – that is, the inevitable preference, willing or choice of higher or lower values in every expression of personality – then everything we do is of some moral consequence.

Perhaps we can clarify the ethical significance of this approach by considering its implications for an abiding ethical dilemma, namely, the question of whether, and if so when, the ends of an action justify the means employed towards its attainment. One of the stronger arguments in favour of this principle contends that means are insignificant when considered apart from their results and that, in the final analysis, it is the goodness or evil of the end which imparts to the means employed whatever ethical status they might have. Here, any resolution of the means–ends problem rests with determining whether or not the end itself can be justi-fied. Thus, the scientific/technological manipulation and control of the physical environment would be a morally neutral practice that one could evaluate only subsequent to the knowledge of whether it were detrimental or beneficial to human life. Those who might attempt to counter this mode of ethical judgement could well respond that the choice of questionable means can corrupt the most noble end, citing the numerous instances in which human beings have set out to implement grand designs, only to discover that in so doing they had violated the very principles they sought to affirm. The example of the revolution which ends up devouring its children is but one disturbing and frequent example.

What is relevant here for our discussion is that both of these responses to the means–ends dilemma presuppose a distance between the morality of the acting subjects on the one hand and the ethical character and consequences of their actions on the other. It is a distance that Scheler would not grant. Once we place the Person squarely within the events that comprise the means-ends continuum a far different set of considerations arise. It is no longer possible to analyse the relationship between means and ends without persistently considering the ethical subject, whether that subject is the individual (*Einzelperson*) or the community (*Socialperson*). This is so, not because we might 'prefer' to make room in our analysis for its immediate human ingredient, but because we *must*: the Person is the universal and necessary correlate (I would prefer to say the 'constant' and 'concrete' source) of all acts, and therefore cannot be left out of the course of our ethical deliberations lest these deliberations evaporate into nonsense.

One result of such a revised or, as I am calling it 'humanised', approach to the means-ends problematic is that the end and moral determinant of any act becomes, not some distant result that can be predicted with varying degrees of certainty but, quite literally, the Person. Recall once more that for Scheler the Person (and, thus, personality) is completely involved in each of its expressions, thereby developing and growing within the dynamic of its own activity. As such each act has immediate and profound implications. For instance, in the previous example the goodness or evil, right or wrong, of technological control of the environment would have to be assessed in terms of its effects upon the Person (individual or collective) involved in the enterprise, rather than in relation to some future consequence for either physical nature or humankind. Indeed, in so far as the future is prepared in the present, it is only in their immediate individual and social consequences that we can have access to the more enduring effects of our actions.

The upshot of these observations is that it is impossible to draw any significant moral distinction between means and ends. Whether we are considering the course of an individual's action or the development of a social policy the moral qualities that will ultimately prevail are being created and moulded in each step and moment along the way. It is an old adage worth repeating: the adult is present in the child. Similarly, the values, practices and institutions that will distinguish any future social order are present at its inception. What we become, in this sense, is what we already are.

This is but one implication of the turn ethical inquiry and discourse takes when the Person assumes a position of central importance in any consideration of the human condition. To be sure, we are moving here beyond the letter of Scheler's philosophical anthropology. However, this move seems consistent with his persistent willingness to pursue his insights into new and uncharted territory. And, as is the case with the work of any seminal thinker, this extension of his thought into the circumstances, problems and possibilities of our own time is warranted by the simple fact that he is unable fully to anticipate how this thought might play out in a different, but not altogether foreign, setting.

This last point is particularly telling for the question of how we might now interpret Scheler's call for a new and 'total' idea of man. While his theoretical conception of the Person leads him ultimately to entertain the possibility of a dramatic transformation in human nature, and while his thoughts take him to the conclusion that some such transformation was necessary to resolve the crisis in Western civilisation, Scheler seems unable to entertain the far more radical prospect that such a transformation might be possible in practice as well as in theory. Yet, I can find no compelling reason that should prevent us from doing so. Indeed, if we are to appraise the full implications of his personalism it seems imperative that we finally move from the realm of pure concepts to the domain of concrete experience.

MAN AND NATURE

Ultimately, Scheler's inability or unwillingness to consider an *actual* transformation of human nature must be ascribed to more than the specific matter of his attachment to Kant's transcendental idealism. So long as our study remains within the general confines of the Kant–Scheler problematic it will remain prejudiced in favour of philosophy, to the exclusion of those other attitudes and activities that comprise the cultural matrix. In short, we will remain oblivious to those anthropological, social and historical factors that have influenced the philosophy of modernity, and ignorant of the extent to which any transformation in the ways of human perception, understanding and experience must involve these very factors.

In an essay entitled 'The Affirmative Character of Culture', Herbert Marcuse provides an excellent starting point for such an historical–cultural assessment by placing the post-Kantian doctrine of the Person in its fuller context. After noting that at the commencement of the modern era (which he dates with the Renaissance) 'the Person was the source of all forces and properties that made the individual capable of mastering his fate and shaping his environment in accordance with his needs', Marcuse notes that,

in the concept of personality which has been representative . . .since Kant, there is nothing left of this expansive activism The personality remains lord of its existence only as a spiritual and ethical subject. 'Freedom and independence from the mechanism of nature as a whole,' which is now the token of its nature, is only an 'intelligible' freedom that accepts the given circumstances of life as the material of duty. Space for external fulfillment has shrunk: space for inner fulfillment has expanded considerably. The individual has learned to place all demands primarily upon himself. The rule of the soul has become more exacting inwardly and more modest outwardly. The person is no longer a springboard for attacking the world, but rather is a protected line of retreat behind the front. In its inwardness, as an ethical person, it is the individual's only secure possession, the only one he can never lose. It is no longer the source of conquest, but of renunciation. Personality characterizes above all him who renounces, who ekes out fulfillment within given conditions, no matter how poor they might be. He finds happiness in the Establishment.[2]

While the immediate references in this passage are to Kant it is clear that Scheler stands squarely within the post-Kantian tradition that Marcuse has in mind. While Scheler's concept of the Person is more expansive than Kant's, it is an 'inward' expansion and, as such, no more activist than Kant's. Scheler too accepts nature as the realm of facticity and consequently can conceive of no transformation – evolutionary or revolutionary – that could either affect or incorporate the presumably immutable laws of nature and the object-world. This was particularly evident when we saw Scheler making the *a priori* claim that the full development of our moral capacity would necessitate a break with the natural *weltanschauung*. (See the discussion of 'The Moral Upsurge and the Whole Man' in chapter 6.) But the same fatalist distinction is present when Scheler turns his attention to that grey area where nature and spirit merge, that is, in the region of human being where we find values and expressions of personality that are vital and organic on the one hand, while intellectual and spiritual on the other. To be sure, Scheler does make passing acknowledgement of the interaction between our natural and intellectual aptitudes. But he ultimately concludes that the former is, indeed, immutable and that any change in Man will have both its origin and its terminus in the realm of the spirit: '*the whole spiritual Person must love absolute value and being; the natural self and ego must be humbled*'. (EM 95)

However, if we are able seriously to question the legitimacy of that entire array of distinctions which confounds Scheler's genuine desire to enrich and concretise our understanding of moral experience, a dramatically different picture might begin to emerge. This would entail the undermining of the ontic and ontological barriers, the 'divided lines' of Occidental philosophy, which have served to distinguish the intellectual from the physical, the inner realm of freedom from the outer world of necessity, the values and goods of the spirit from those of the body, and the Apollonian from the Dionysian; barriers that, in their cumulative effect, leave us with the image of a humanity twice estranged: from the nature which lies within us as well as that which stands beyond us.

Admittedly it is easier for us today to question the validity of these pernicious dualisms than it was when Scheler turned his attention to the need to do so in his address to the German Institute for Politics at Berlin. For one, he did not have the psychological and anthropological studies at his disposal that have since indicated how the natural–physical dimensions of both human and extra-human existence are much more fluid than the traditional dichotomies and dualisms would allow, and that changes in these environments can and do induce remarkable alterations in the sphere of consciousness.

We will recall that at one point Scheler entertains the possibility of a redistribution of energy between the cortex and the rest of the human organism, a possibility his subsequent reflections are unable to sustain. Yet one, more recent, study on the effect of electrical stimulation of the brain may indicate that far more of that organ is capable of eliciting pleasurable (or rewarding) effects than is capable of eliciting repressive (or punishing) effects. (A capacity, we should note, that has not yet been manifested by anything approaching a majority of humankind). While these results were achieved under artificial conditions the author felt justified in drawing two conclusions that are relevant here. First, the physical propensities and functions of the brain are not fixed and immutable. On the contrary, there is a 'predominance of the potential for pleasurable sensations'. Second, in an observation that suggests *empirical* confirmation of Scheler's *eidetic* account of the developing Person, the author concludes that 'personality is not an intangible, immutable way of reacting but a flexible process in continuous evolution, *affected by its medium*'.[3] Perhaps the appropriate image by which we might discriminate between our physical and intellectual capacities is not the divided line, but the permeable membrane!

But we need not resort to controlled and artificial means to suggest that Scheler's failure to overcome the rigid demarcation between the respective domains of the physical and the intellectual is not conclusive. From his studies of the development of intelligence in children Jean Piaget concluded that its origins are indistinguishable from those of sensory-motor adaptation in general, or even from those of biological adaptation itself.

> Furthermore, intelligence itself does not consist of an isolated and sharply differentiated class of cognitive processes. It is not, strictly speaking, one form of structuring among others; it is the form of equilibrium towards which all the structures arising out of perception, habit and elementary sensory-motor mechanisms tend. It must be understood that if intelligence is not a faculty, this denial involves a radical functional continuity between the higher forms of thought and the whole mass of lower types of cognitive and motor adaptation. . . [4]

Some 20 years after the publication of *The Psychology of Intelligence*, Maria Montessori echoed Piaget with her insistence that 'the education of the senses' is a necessary prelude to any 'higher' form of intellectual activity.

> Our aim in education in general is two-fold, biological and social. From the biological side we wish to help the natural development of the individual, from the social standpoint it is our aim to prepare the individual for the environment. . .The education of the senses is most important from both these points of view. The development of the senses indeed precedes that of superior intellectual activity and the child between three and seven years is in the period of formation . . . The stimuli, and not yet the reasons for things, attract his attention. This is, therefore, the time when we should methodically direct the sense stimuli, in such a way that the sensations he receives shall develop in a rational way. This sense training will prepare the ordered formation upon which he may build up a clear and strong mentality.[5]

A cursory reading of this passage might suggest that this radical innovation in the educational process does little more than prepare the child for a passive adjustment to his or her environment. However, the results suggest otherwise. Inspired by the example of Helen Keller, Montessori achieved remarkable success in enabling children to *overcome* what many would have considered insurmountable physical handicaps.

It is, besides all this, possible with the education of the senses to correct defects which today pass unobserved in the school. Now the time comes when the defect manifests itself in an evident and irreparable inability to make use of the forces of life about him. (Such defects as deafness and near-sightedness.) This education, therefore, is physiological and prepares directly for intellectual education, perfecting the organs of sense, and the nerve-paths of projection and association.[6]

These findings suggest that to recognise an inextricable link between the organic-sensual and the intellectual-spiritual aspects of human nature need not necessarily compromise our freedom by reducing us to the status of physical objects, subject to immutable physical laws. On the contrary, Delgado, Piaget and Montessori indicate that through the rational-moral organisation of the physical environment the realm of a self-determined freedom can be expanded to include features of human existence that have previously been taken as unalterable.

Thus, Montessori's work achieved a transformation in her children from individuals whose characters seemed to be fundamentally aggressive to young people who amazed the visitors at 'Children's House' by their calm and peaceful demeanour.

By the substitution of a series of outbursts of *joy* for the old series of outbursts of *rage*, the moral physiognomy of the child comes to assume a calm and gentleness which make him appear to be a different being. It is we who provoked the children to the violent manifestations of a real *struggle for existence*. In order to exist *according to the needs of their psychic development* they were often obliged to snatch from us the things which seemed necessary to them for the purpose. They had to move contrary to our laws, or sometimes to struggle with other children to wrest from them the objects of their desire. On the other hand, if we give children the *means of existence*, the struggle for it disappears, and a vigorous expansion of life takes its place.[7]

The expansion of life that is envisioned here stands in dramatic contrast to that 'inner expansion' Marcuse cites as the hallmark of the modern (post-Kantian) concept of the Person. No longer is it necessary to harbour the values and the acting subject of Scheler's personalist humanism within the safe and untouchable confines of some variant of philosophical idealism. Montessori's work suggests that these themes might at last find their expression within the full course of daily life.

> The child may be said to link two adult generations or, put somewhat differently, two periods of history. To raise the level of man's functioning, to usher in a new cultural era, the unique learning capacities of childhood must be utilized. It is in the child, not the adult, that Montessori sees the hope for the emergence of a new mankind tantamount to a new race of 'spiritual men' capable of achieving a new plane of ethics to which man already strives, however falteringly. The potential then, for a 'new man' is in the child, whose development in all spheres – physical, emotional, intellectual, social, and spiritual – needs safeguarding and the optimal nourishment made possible in a 'prepared environment'.[8]

It is, of course, impossible to overstate the importance of the role played by the physical-social environment in Piaget and Montessori. For if the developed forms of intellectual activity are in large measure shaped, moulded and directed by biological states that are inevitably contextualised within a setting of social stimuli and responses, then those philosophies that take up with the various manifestations of the intellect – ethics, science and so on – as if they resided in some autonomous and timeless realm of thought, can never achieve an adequate comprehension of their subject matter. Any adequate understanding of these distinctive expressions of our humanity would have to be grounded in reflections upon those 'enabling environments' – the physical, social and the political – and, particularly, upon those situations which find women and men in seemingly pre-cognitive and 'natural' relationships within those environments.

To be sure, there are few who would deny, at least in theory, the influence of the natural, organic and social contexts of human experience on our cognitive and intellectual development. However, as we have seen with both Kant and Scheler, attempts fully to acknowledge and explore that influence can be short-circuited by an unspoken concession to the premiss that there is some impassable gap between those structures of experience which, by virtue of their physical origins – that is, their proximity with the 'lower' natural order human beings share with other forms of organic and sentient life – are immutable, and those aspects of experience which arise within the course of conscious reflection and are thereby subject to the determinations of reason and will.

At this point readers might well object that the case I am trying to make for the possible transformation of what seem to be fixed attributes of human nature relies too exclusively upon those figures who stand on one side of an ongoing debate over the relative weight we ought to assign to nurture v. nature in our understanding of personal development. In conventional representations of this debate Piaget and Montessori would stand on the 'nurture' side, a position that presumably fuels their optimistic appraisal of what human beings are yet capable of. But this statement of the matter is, in my judgement, a misrepresentation of what is intended with the studies I have cited. If we consider the work of two apparent antagonists of authors like Piaget and Montessori, work which presumably supports the pessimists' account of human nature, it should be clear that a genuine account of personal development cannot be derived from an either-or-setting in which either fixed laws of nature or the dynamic influence of the natural-social environment hold sway. Quite the contrary, whether we turn to the 'optimists' or the 'pessimists', the picture that emerges is more complex: one which describes a dialectical relationship of reciprocal influence between the physical-social environment on the one hand and what Scheler described as the intellectual-spiritual domain on the other.

THE DYNAMIC OF AGGRESSION

In what seems to be profoundly contrary to the findings of Piaget and Montessori, the school of thought pioneered by Robert Ardrey and Konrad Lorenz claims to see no possibility for the ultimate displacement of the more aggressive features of human nature.

The Lorenz approach to human aggression is, first, that it

is healthy, that it is necessary, that it is innate, that it is ineradicable; second, that the solution to the human problem *is to be sought in an imitation of nature*, in other words, by the enlargement of all those less-than-lethal competitions, ritualizations and displays, whether between individuals or groups, which absorb our hostile energies and turn them to ends either harmless or constructive; and, finally, that to deny the innateness of human aggression is to approach its possible control from an inevitably impossible quarter, that to accept its cause as lying in frustration is to lend hostility moral sanction, and to turn its more virulent, antisocial, antisurvival forces loose on a defenseless world.[9]

It is important to note that in this version of *realanthropology*, whose implications for *realpolitik* are resonant in Ardrey's account, the reference to an 'imitation of nature' does not signify the domain of the natural or 'physical' sciences. Instead, Lorenz is looking to the arena in which the various species of animal-life hold sway. And, his study therein of 'the natural history of aggression' leads him to conclude that in order to ensure their survival some species have developed specific patterns of behaviour which satisfy the aggressive 'drive' while simultaneously furthering the needs of the larger society. Thus, in the case of aggression between individuals:

> The injury-preventing rites of threatening and the subsequent measuring of strength represent, in their original form, only an elaborate introduction of the real, ruthless battle. But such a prolonged introduction fulfills an extremely important function, in that it enables the weaker rival to withdraw in time from a hopeless contest. Thus in most cases the species-preserving function of the rival fight, selection of the stronger, is fulfilled without the loss or even the wounding of one of the individuals.[10]

On the face of it, this does not seem to be a particularly remarkable observation. The striking feature of Lorenz's thesis only becomes apparent when he turns to the human implications of his study. There he assigns primacy to the aggressive drive in the development of attributes that seem to be far removed from the more belligerent expressions of personality, attributes to which Scheler assigned the status of 'positive values' and sought to locate within the timeless sphere of the Person. For example, Lorenz contends that personal love and friendship appear in human evolution only when it becomes necessary for two or more members of an aggressive species to unite for survival against the threats of a hostile environment or the aggressive intentions of other members of the same species.

> Intra-specific aggression is millions of years older than personal friendship and love. During long epochs of the earth's history, there have been animals that were certainly extraordinarily fierce and aggressive. Nearly all reptiles of the present day are aggressive and it is unlikely that those of antiquity were less so. But the personal bond is known only in certain teleost fishes, birds, and mammals, that is in groups that did not appear before the Tertiary period. Thus intra-specific aggression can certainly exist without its counterpart, love, but conversely *there is no love without aggression*.[11]

Lorenz, then, assigns to love and friendship, as well as ritualised combat, (and a host of other expressions ranging from laughter to enthusiasm) the status of 'inhibitory mechanisms' that have evolved as ever higher species strove to find legitimate and relatively safe outlets for their aggressions. Consequently, we should not be surprised to find him cashing in on his thinly disguised anthropocentric portrayal of species-life with a paradox. The 'imitation of nature' which he enjoins us to affect would take shape in a global ritualisation of our hostilities within non-lethal structures, in order to establish a future in which 'love and friendship should embrace all humanity', and 'in which we should love all our human brothers indiscriminately'.[12]

LIMITED TRANSFORMATIONS

At this point it is difficult to determine who are the optimists and who the pessimists; those who highlight the benevolent capacities of human beings or those who dwell upon the aggressive. But neither this, nor a detailed assessment of their specific claims, is the intent of my inquiry. What I have been concerned to accomplish is far more modest, yet, perhaps, not insignificant. Piaget,

Montessori and Lorenz invite us to take seriously the radically open vision of human experience – of personal and collective development – that emerges when the matrix of physical and social environments is assigned its dialectical place in the process of moral cognition and practice. Against Scheler's depiction of a fixed hierarchy of values (whose higher reaches are accessible to only a philosophical élite and are obscured by the respective systems of morality displayed in history) the psychologist, the educator and the anthropologist – in these instances, at least – portray a situation of fluid reciprocity between consciousness and nature, a situation in which the non-human as well as the social environments reflect what humankind (understood as a moral and rational agency) has accomplished and, in complementary fashion, delineates both the possibilities and boundaries of what may yet come to be.

Subsequently, when we situate the central terms of Scheler's personalist philosophical anthropology within the practical context I have been describing, a different sense of human transformation becomes available. The prospects of such a transformation as that enjoined by Scheler are not confined to the realm of the intellect and spirit alone. Nor, and I consider this a crucial point, does the possibility of such a transformation rest upon the ability to envisage a total break with the naturalist *Weltanschauung*. When we reinsert Scheler's problematic back into nature and history a more humble, but no less imperative, task emerges. It is not that of elaborating yet another programme for a 'new man' – with all the totalising, authoritarian and élitist implications such projects entail – but one of developing moral and practical responses to the great changes now occurring within the human condition, as well as between humankind and its fragile habitats: the ecological no less than the social and the political. As Michel Foucault puts it, 'I prefer the very specific transformations that have proved to be possible in the last twenty years in a certain number of areas that concern our ways of being and thinking, relations to authority, relations between the sexes, the way in which we perceive insanity or illness; I prefer even the partial transformations that have been made in the correlation of historical analysis and the practical attitude, to the programs for a new man that the worst political systems have repeated throughout the twentieth century'.[13] But if it is the case that by attending more closely to what I have chosen to describe as the 'dialectic' which obtains between the things of the spirit and the things of the world, we might begin addressing ourselves (as Scheler could not) to the manner in which humankind might continue to transform itself, it may yet be the case that our philosopher will have the last word. For the question persists: in what temper might these transformations be accomplished and what ends and visions might inspire them? Here, perhaps, our brief study of Scheler and of Kant before him might again be instructive.

Throughout Part Two of this study we have observed a tension in Scheler's thought between, on the one hand, the residual concerns of enlightenment humanism for the power of human reason and the autonomy of will and, on the other, a unique affirmation of the human prospect that privileges the experience of values and the normative expressions of human personality. Again and again, we have seen his most seminal and provocative insights compromised by his allegiance to post-Kantian conceptions of the Person and Nature. This uneasy pattern suggests that if philosophy and the philosopher are to play a role in those profound changes that now range across the entire spectrum of what Scheler calls 'the modalities of values', they will do so the extent to which they are able to effect a radical break with the received conceptions of human nature; of the relationships that obtain between human beings and their natural-physical surroundings, as well as those which obtain between individuals and society. Here, by a 'radical' break I have in mind: (1) the will to achieve some cognitive distance from the tired, clichéd, and ideologically encased presumptions that govern our understandings of human nature; (2) the capacity to assess critically the significance of these presumptions in relation to the cultures and times that they represented; and (3) the ability to expand our intellectual horizons by embracing the ongoing studies of the human condition undertaken by those who are often far removed from the professional world of philosophy.[14]

But the adoption of the stance I am advocating cannot and does not imply the desire or ability to dump all the understandings and values of the past into the dustbin of history. Indeed, the very idea of a questioning that accepts no doctrine or practice at face value is itself, we should recall, a deep, abiding and traditional value of philosophical inquiry. It is, indeed, the unspoken value that informed Scheler's decision to examine the presuppositions of Kant's own system of critical philosophy. If the present study has sought to reveal anything it is not that this was anything less than a noble intention, but that his failure to move decisively beyond Kant was the result of Scheler's inability to sustain the radical-critical course upon which he embarked.

Conversely, his most challenging claims and observations appear at those moments when he does succeed in distancing himself from the root assumptions of Kant and the tradition of thought he initiated. Perhaps the most notable of these challenges is a feature of Scheler's refusal to accept any definitive distinction between the form and content of the experience of values. This enables him to introduce a whole new dimension into the systematic study of ethics. It is this that might serve us well as we deliberate over the ends and interests which might guide the partial transformations to which Foucault refers.

Whether or not Scheler finally 'gets it right' with his insistence that the phenomenological consideration of value structures and relationships reveal their *a priori* characteristics is not of lasting importance. What is important is his enriching of our moral understanding by expanding the language of ethical discourse into a domain recently seen as beyond the pale of serious reflection and inquiry. Not since the decline of the Aristotelean moral tradition have we encountered a philosopher who insisted that the full range of normative experience can and must be available to serious intellectual inquiry. His willingness and capacity to confront this experience – from those moments in which we are affected by the pleasurable or the distasteful, to those in which we collectively strive to affirm our common interests in personal dignity and social well-being – are in striking contrast to those limited, fragmentary and cautious depictions of the moral life that have been predominant in ethical studies since the philosophers of modernity began to drive their cognitive wedge between the normative and descriptive features of human experience.

But there is more to be said in defence of the course Scheler would set for us. If he has a strong claim upon our philosophical attentions today it is because of the mounting evidence that we are entering the age of what many are increasingly characterising as 'post-modernity', with an attitude akin to that of Dostoievski's Ivan Karamazov. Except, in our instance it is not the sense that God is dead that leads to the suspicion that 'everything is permitted'. Rather it is the fear that there are no common patterns to be found in the midst of our competing tastes, desires and interests. For the individual human being this translates into a moral solipsism wherein the only conceivable locus for ethical judgements is the individual's preferences and intentions. For societies and nations it translates into a new version of the doctrine that 'might makes right', a doctrine against which moral philosophy has struggled since Plato's Socrates confronted Thrasymachus in *The Republic*.

Alasdair MacIntyre has aptly described and assessed this present climate in the terms of an 'emotivism' in which 'the sole reality of distinctively moral discourse is the attempt of one will to align the attitudes, feelings, preferences and choices of another with its own'. In such a context, he correctly notes, 'others are always means, never ends'.[15] By reminding us that one of the signal features of moral sensibility is the ability to perceive the substance of personality as the end which lies within the deeds and cares of women, men, children, communities and societies, Scheler provides us with a rich alternative to that demoralising and instrumental image of human relationships.

Notes

Preface

1. Throughout this study I have opted to capitalise the noun 'man' to indicate a gender-free reference to the species, when the use of such expressions as 'he or she' and 'humankind' would be unnecessarily awkward.
2. Lewis Mumford, *The City in History* (New York: Harcourt, Brace and World, 1961), 4.

Introduction

1. Hereafter all references to this work will be cited in my text with the abbreviation FORM followed by the page number. All such citations will be to the third edition published in Bern by Franke Verlag in 1966. Unless otherwise noted all translations are mine. Readers who do not have access to the German text are advised to consult the English translation by Manfred S. Frings and Roger L. Funk: Max Scheler, *Formalism in Ethics and Non-Formal Ethics of Values: A New Attempt toward the Foundation of an Ethical Personalism* (Evanston: Illinois: Northwestern University Press, 1973).
2. While Frings and Funk have chosen to translate *materiale* as 'non-formal', my sense is that this locution is both too inclusive and too negative. Many philosophical ethics could be loosely described as non-formal. What is more, to characterise Scheler's effort in terms of what it is not may obscure his concern to establish a distinctive and affirmative foundation for ethics in the experience of an *a priori* order of values that formal, ethical systems such as Kant's, deny.
3. See Manfred S. Frings, *Max Scheler, A Concise Introduction Into the World of a Great Thinker* (Pittsburgh: Duquesne University Press, 1965), p. 105. This work is recommended as a concise, yet comprehensive, introduction to the variety of Scheler's philosophical endeavours.
4. Derek Parfit, *Reasons and Persons* (Oxford: Clarendon Press, 1984).
5. See T. W. Adorno *et al.*, *The Authoritarian Personality* (New York: W. W. Norton and Co., 1950) and Fred I. Greenstein, *Personality and Politics* (Chicago: Markham, 1969). The Greenstein includes a fine survey of related literature in a 'Bibliographical Note' by Michael Lerner.
6. Foucault reminds us that there have been many varieties of humanism. 'In the seventeenth century, there was a humanism that presented itself as a critique of Christianity or of religion in general; there was a Christian humanism opposed to an ascetic and much more theocentric humanism. In the nineteenth century there was a suspicious humanism, hostile and critical toward science,

and another that, to the contrary, placed its hope in the same science. Marxism has been a humanism, so have existentialism and personalism; there was a time when people supported the humanistic values represented by National Socialism, and when the Stalinists themselves said they were humanists'. Michel Foucault, 'What is Enlightenment', in *The Foucault Reader*, ed. Paul Rabinow (New York: Pantheon Books, 1984), p. 44.

1 The Ethical Implications of Kant's First Critique

1. Thomas Kingsley Abbott, tr., *Kant's Critique of Practical Reason and Other Works on the Theory of Ethics* (London: Longman's, Green, 1909), p. 44.
2. Ibid., p. 107
3. Norman Kemp Smith, tr., *Immanuel Kant's Critique of Pure Reason* (London: Macmillan, 1963). Hereafter, unless noted otherwise, all references will be to this edition and cited in the text by the pagination of Kant's first (A) and second (B) editions.
4. Norman Kemp Smith, *A Commentary to Kant's Critique of Pure Reason*, 2nd. edn. (New York: Humanities Press, reprinted by special arrangement with Macmillan, 1962), p. 18.
5. Ibid., p. 23.
6. This statement seems inconsistent with my earlier contention that, strictly speaking, objects are the result of an act of concept- ualisation, and not given in intuition. In support of my governing interpretation *vis-à-vis* the conceptual v intuitive status of objectivity, I would cite Norman Kemp Smith's observation that Kant often uses the term *Objekt* in its 'widest and most indefinite meaning', and that in the context of empirical intuition it may be taken to signify the content of intuition (ibid., p. 79). This is the meaning which I believe best suits its use here. Smith also points out that when Kant responded to Jacob Beck's objection that 'only through subsumption under the categories can a representation become objective', Kant sought to clarify himself by noting that what is given in empirical intuition is a content which is *due* to some object' (my emphasis) (ibid., p. 81).

 With this last observation Kant is referring to the thing-in-itself which is represented in those judgements that yield empirical knowledge but never present in experience as it is in itself, that is, as 'an object in general'.
7. Friedrich Nietzsche, *The Will to Power*, tr. Walter Kaufmann and R. J. Hollingdale, ed., Walter Kaufmann (New York: Random House, 1967), p. 35.
8. Smith translates *Naturursachen* as 'natural causes'. Since the term clearly means 'natural things', I can only presume that at this point the text is corrupt.
9. It is worth noting that the image of Man which emerges here reflects the attitude of liberal-democratic society towards the

'criminal'. There we find a recognition that behind his or her actions one can establish a series of causal events, for instance, an environment of social deprivation. Simultaneously, however, we find the claim that he or she is responsible and, with the criminal trial, enact the assumption that he or she *ought* to have known the difference between good and evil.

Kant too made reference to this ambiguity although he offered it as illustration, rather than proof, of his argument. (A 554, B 582 – A 555, B 583).

10. John Silber, 'The Ethical Significance of Kant's Religion', in Kant, *Religion Within the Limits of Reason Alone*, tr. Theodore M. Greene and Hoyt H. Hudson (New York: Harper & Row, 1960), cii.
11. Ibid., cii.

2 The Formal Ethics

1. Norman Kemp Smith, *A Commentary*, pp. 572–3.
2. Immanuel Kant, *Kritik der Practischen Vernunft* (Hamburg: Felix Meiner, 1963), pp. 39–40. All translations from this edition are mine.
3. Ibid., p. 34.
4. Ibid., p. 4.
5. Ibid., pp. 36–8.
6. Ibid., p. 38.
7. Silber, 'The Ethical Significance', xciv.
8. Kant, *Kritik*, p. 39. Unless we recognise that, for Kant, the autonomy of the will, Reason's ability to determine itself in accord with principles that are uniquely its own (namely, formal principles), and the positive notion of freedom constitute a single cluster of meaning, his reciprocal use of these terms can become needlessly confusing.
9. Silber, 'The Ethical Significance', xcviii-xcix.
10. Ibid., xcv-xcvi.
11. Ibid., civ.
12. Ibid., xcviii.
13. Abbott, *Kant's Critique of Practical Reason*, p. 121.
14. Ibid., cii.
15. Ibid., cii.
16. Kant, *Kritik*, p. 50.
17. Abbott, *Kant's Critique of Practical Reason*, p. 132. Here, it should be noted that Kant's reference to a 'pure world of understanding' is to the intelligible world and not to the world of experience over which the Understanding holds sway in the first *Critique*.
18. Ibid., p. 135.
19. *The Works of Aristotle*, tr. under the direction of W. D. Ross, (Oxford: Oxford University Press, 1930), vol. 2, *Physica*, 194b 25–198b 5.
20. Kant, *Kritik*, p. 83. In order to avoid being misled by Kant's allusions to the 'reality' of the 'objects' of the moral law and

practical Reason, it is worth reminding ourselves that what is intended here is not spacial-temporal existence but, rather, ideal reality. As one study points out, 'freedom is real only to the same extent, and in the same sense, as Reason is real'. See, Wilhelm Teichner, *Die Intelligible Welt* (Anton Hain: Meisenheim am Glan, 1967), p. 112.

21. Kant, *Kritik*, pp. 97 and 137.
22. Ibid., p. 85.
23. Ibid., p. 86.
24. See, *Hegel's Phenomenology of Spirit*, tr. A. V. Miller, analysis of the text and foreword by J. N. Findlay (Oxford: Oxford University Press, 1977), pp. 355–63.
25. Kant, *Kritik*, p. 88.
26. Abbott, *Kant's Critique of Practical Reason*, pp. 171–2.
27. Kant, *Kritik*, p. 94.
28. Abbott, *Kant's Critique of Practical Reason*, p. 175.
29. Ibid., p. 51.
30. Kant, *Kritik*, p. 89.
31. Ibid., p. 101.
32. Ibid., p. 102.
33. Ibid., p. 91.
34. Teichner, *Die Intelligible Welt*, p. 121.
35. Kant, *Religion Within the Limits*, p. 23.
36. Immanuel Kant, *Lectures on Ethics*, tr. Louis Infield, foreword by Lewis White Beck (New York: Harper & Row Torchbook, 1963), p. 23.
37. Kant, *Kritik*, pp. 94 and 102.
38. Kant, *Religion Within the Limits*, p. 42–3.
39. Ibid., p. 43.
40. Ibid., p. 43.
41. Immanuel Kant, 'The Critique of Teleological Judgement', in Kant, *The Critique of Judgement*, tr. James Creed Meredith (Oxford: Oxford University Press), p. 20.
42. Ibid., p. 99.
43. Ibid., p. 124.
44. Ibid., pp. 113–4.

3 Scheler, Phenomenology and the Two Orders of Reason

1. John Raphael Staude, *Max Scheler: An Intellectual Portrait* (New York: The Free Press, 1967), p. 27.
2. The examples of private property and the state are mine. More often than not, Scheler does not provide us with ample illustrations which might help to clarify his intent.
3. Frings, *Max Scheler*, p. 131.
4. Max Scheler, *Die Wissensformen und die Gesellschaft*, ed. Maria Scheler, in Scheler, *Gesammelte Werke*, 13 vols. (Bern: Franke Verlag, 1954 –), 8: pp. 109–10.

5. Edmund Husserl, *Ideas: General Introduction to Pure Phenomenology*, tr. W. Boyce Gibson (New York: Collier, 1962), p. 101.
6. Ibid., pp. 99–100.
7. The effect of the *epoche* may be compared to that of a close-up in film, particularly when this is achieved by means of a zoom lens. At one moment the subject is but one element within the surrounding landscape, perhaps eluding the viewer's attention as the eye wanders across the screen. Then, as the camera focuses in, the subject fills the entire field of vision with each of its features etched in sharp detail.
8. Paul Ricoeur, *Husserl, An Analysis of His Phenomenology* (Evanston: Northwestern University Press, 1967), p. 17.
9. Moritz Geiger, 'Zu Max Scheler's Tod', *Vorrische Zeitung*, 1 June 1928. Cited and translated in Herbert Spiegelberg, *The Phenomenological Movement*, 2 vols. (The Hague: Martinus Nijhoff, 1965), 1: p. 236.
10. Spiegelberg, *The Phenomenological Movement*, 1: p. 240.
11. Here, any literal translation of the German text is bound to be misleading. Therefore, I have exercised some licence in an effort to present a statement that might read clearly and smoothly in English. The original text reads: 'Als Apriori bezeichnen wir alle jene idealen Bedeutungseinheiten und Satze, die unter Absehen von jeder Art von Setzung der sie denkenden Subjecte und ihrer realen Naturbeschaffenheit und unter Absehen von jeder Art von Setzung eines Gegenständes, auf den sie anwendbar waren, durch den Gehalt einer *unmittelbaren Anschauung* zur Selbstgegebenheit kommen'.
12. See, for example, Rev. Marius Schneider, *Max Scheler's Phenomenological Philosophy of Values* (PhD diss., Catholic University, 1953), p. 176, and Robert D. Sweeny, *Max Scheler's Philosophy of Values* (PhD diss., Fordham University, 1962).

4 Scheler's Hierarchy of Values

1. Here Scheler has deliberately rendered the German verbs *vorziehen* and *nachsetzen* as nouns in order to treat the act of setting greater or lesser values upon a thing, state or event, as a phenomenon. In part, this move has its English-language equivalent in the verb-noun relationship between 'prefer' and 'preference'. However, a clear complement for *nachsetzen* is more difficult to render. I have chosen 'depreciation' as one approximation, rather than adopting the clumsy, but more literal, locution, 'placed after'.
2. While Scheler does not explicitly recall this earlier argument, his comments here would be unduly arbitrary if he had not already distinguished between values and goods.
3. Nicolai Hartmann, *Ethics*, tr., Stanton Coit, 3 vols. (London: Allen & Unwin, 1932), 2: p. 284.
4. For an interesting criticism of Scheler's third criterion see,

Hartmann, *Ethics*, 2: pp. 26–9. Hartmann agrees with Scheler that the values of utility are dependent, as means, upon some further end. But he correctly points out that Scheler generalises from this one instance to a teleology that would make all lower values, for instance, the biological, dependent on higher values. In chapter 5 we shall have occasion to consider further what Hartmann terms Scheler's 'teleological prejudice'.

5. In suggesting that there may be some methodological justification for Scheler's position, I do not intend to exempt it from criticism. Indeed, this seems to be one clear instance of Scheler's propensity to claim too much for phenomenological intuition. However, any detailed analysis should wait upon a further elaboration of his scheme of values.

6. See, Stephen Frederick Schneck, *Person and Polis: Max Scheler's Personalism as Political Theory* (Albany: State University of New York Press, 1987), pp. 38–9.

7. Throughout this discussion it is important to bear in mind that each rank or modality of values will range across a spectrum of normative experience that extends from its positive to its negative expressions. See the discussion of the 'Material *a Priori*' in chapter 3.

8. John Stuart Mill, *Utilitarianism, Liberty, and Representative Government* (London: J. M. Dent, 1910), p. 6.

9. See especially, Chapter Three, 'Hedonism', in G. E. Moore, *Principia Ethica* (Cambridge: The University Press, 1962).

10. As a preliminary observation to the fuller discussion of chapter 5, we can note that the distinction Scheler draws here between the Person and the Ego reflects considerations similar to those which prompted Kant to cite the concept of personality in denoting Man's unique moral capacity. As such, the concept of Person has a far more specific meaning for both philosophers than could be captured with the general designation, 'ego'.

11. In a later work Scheler becomes more definitive by suggesting that in the figure of the saint – who most closely approximates the absolute by creating himself 'in accordance with a value image which he has acquired in the act of loving himself only "in God" ' – we find the clearest personal prototype of the holy. 'The *saint* is the person most independent of extrinsic material, in that his "work" is none other than "himself" or the souls of other men, who in voluntary emulation reproduce afresh his work's ideal content of meaning and value – that is, his own spiritual pattern and figure'. Max Scheler, *On the Eternal in Man*, tr. Bernard Noble (New York: Harper & Row, 1960), p. 222.

12. See the discussion of 'Scheler and Phenomenology', in chapter 3.

13. Edmund Husserl, 'Philosophy as Rigorous Science', in *Phenomenology and the Crisis of Philosophy*, tr. with notes and an introduction by Quentin Lauer (New York: Harper & Row, 1965), p. 106.

14. Spiegelberg, *The Phenomenological Movement*, 1: p. 266.

15. Frings, *Max Scheler*, p. 125.
16. See the discussion of 'The Transcendental Idea of Freedom' in chapter 1. In drawing this parallel I am presuming the reader's recollection of the differences between Kant and Scheler that were discussed at length in chapter 3: specifically, Scheler's concern with the whole of value experience rather than its pure legislative aspects, and his attempt to deal with the content of that experience within the context of material *a priori* knowledge.
17. Frings, *Max Scheler*, p. 125.

5 The Person

1. Spiegelberg, *The Phenomenological Movement*, 1: p. 125.
2. The distinction here between *Erleben* and *Erlebnisse* is well illustrated by Wilfred Hartmann in his essay, 'Max Scheler's Theory of Person', *Philosophy Today*, Vol.xii, No. 4/4 (Winter 1968): pp. 246–51. Hartmann cites 'hearing' as a functional experience that can be subjected to quantitative analysis and the act of 'listening to' as the corresponding qualitative experience. The latter is what Scheler has in mind when he refers to *Erleben*. It is to these types of experience that we must turn in order to locate the Person.
3. Schneck, *Person and Polis*, pp. 138–9.
4. Abbott, *Kant's Critique of Practical Reason*, p. 151.
5. The most ambitious and plausible example of this approach is Alasdair MacIntyre's *After Virtue* (Notre Dame, Indiana: University of Notre Dame Press, 1984). See, especially, Chapter Fourteen, 'The Nature of the Virtues'.
6. Max Scheler, *Zur Ethik und Erkenntnislehre*, ed. Maria Scheler (Berlin: Neue Geist Verlag, 1933).
7. Max Scheler, *Philosophical Perspectives*, tr. Oscar A. Haac (Boston: Beacon Press, 1958).
8. Max Scheler, *The Nature of Sympathy*, tr. Peter Heath with a 'General Introduction to Max Scheler's Work' by W. Stark (London: Routledge & Kegan Paul, 1954), pp. 229–30.
9. Ibid., pp. 234–5.

6 The Primacy of Philosophical Experience

1. Here I follow the lead of Bernard Noble, the translator of *Vom Ewigen im Menschen*, in rendering *Aufschwung* as 'upsurge', rather than 'elevation'. The former term, as we shall see, best captures Scheler's intention to describe a movement in thought which thrusts and carries Man out of the naturalistic environment towards an intellectual contemplation of essential reality. Noble's translation is remarkably smooth and accurate. Therefore, all references to this work will be to the English-language edition. However, when there might be some undue ambiguity as a result of Scheler's original choice of terms, I will follow the procedure already adopted and

insert the original German in parentheses. All references to *The Eternal in Man* will be cited in the text with EM and the appropriate pagination.

2. This passage serves as a healthy corrective to the many charges of anti-intellectualism that have been levelled against Scheler.

3. In support of my contention that Scheler has been moving towards a position that can be meaningfully interpreted within the context of transcendental philosophy, it is worth noting that here he explicitly states that the essences of which he speaks occupy a space in the 'transcendental sphere'. (EM 103)

4. As evidence for the fact that this dualism ultimately prevails in Scheler's thought I would further cite the dichotomy in one of his last works (*Die Stellung des Menschen im Kosmos*) between absolute being, God and spirit – here used interchangeably – on the one hand; and life, power, or existence, on the other. This work has been translated as *Man's Place in Nature* by Hans Meyerhoff (Boston: Beacon Press, 1961).

   It should be noted that other readers of Scheler contend he does overcome the dualisms and dichotomies I have been highlighting. A representative instance of this position is Arthur B. Luther's 'The Articulated Unity of Being in Scheler's Phenomenology. Basic Drive and Spirit', in *Max Scheler (1874–1928) Centennial Essays*, ed. Manfred S. Frings (The Hague: Martinus Nijhoff, 1974).

   Luther presents an arguable case for the claim that Scheler's philosophical anthropology describes Man as the lived tension between 'two fundamental articulations of Being: *Drang* (the 'basic drive or thrust' that is characteristic of inorganic as well as organic nature) and *Geist* (spirit). While I have some sympathy for Luther's observation that this is not to be understood as a Cartesian dualism I would note that Luther himself observes that *Drang* and spirit are not reducible to one another. Further, as we have seen repeatedly in this study, Scheler clearly privileges the values of the spirit over the vital values of bodily life.

5. This is not to suggest that Scheler and Kant are as one on this issue. I will consider the differences between their positions at greater length in the final chapter.

6. This essay has been published in Scheler, *Philosophical Perspectives*. Hereafter all references to this work will be cited in the text as 'PP' followed by the appropriate pagination.

7 Towards a Radical Humanism

1. See Jürgen Habermas, 'The Entwinement of Myth and Enlightenment: Horkheimer and Adorno', in Habermas, *The Philosophical Discourse of Modernity*, tr. Frederick Lawrence (Cambridge, Mass.: The MIT Press, 1987) and 'Some Consequences of the Failure of the Project', in MacIntyre, *After Virtue*.

2. Herbert Marcuse, *Negations* (Boston: Beacon Press, 1968), pp. 123–4.

3.   Jose M. R. Delgado, 'ESB', *Psychology Today* vol. 3, no. 12 (May 1970), pp. 51, 53.
4.   Jean Piaget, *The Psychology of Intelligence* (London: Routledge & Kegan Paul, 1947), pp. 6–7. Piaget's is no crude behaviourism. In fact, his claim that 'intelligence appears only with acts of insight' is much closer to the spirit of Scheler's thought than it is to any current behavioural representations of the cognitive process.
5.   Maria Montessori, *The Montessori Method* (Cambridge, Mass.: Bentley, 1967), pp. 215–16.
6.   Ibid., pp. 216–17.
7.   R. C. Orem, ed., *A Montessori Handbook*. 'Dr. Montessori's Own Handbook' (New York: G. P. Putnam, 1965), p. 160.
8.   Ibid., p. 15.
9.   Robert Ardrey, *The Territorial Imperative* (New York: Athenium, 1967), p. 302.
10. Konrad Lorenz, *On Aggression* (New York: Harcourt, Brace and World, 1966), p. 113.
11. Ibid., p. 217.
12. Ibid., p. 299.
13. Foucault, 'What is Enlightenment', pp. 46–7.
14. In our time the most ambitious effort towards this comprehensive end is that of Habermas. See especially, *The Theory of Communicative Action*, vol. 1, *Reason and the Rationalization of Society*, tr. Thomas McCarthy (Boston: Beacon Press, 1981) and vol. 2, *Lifeworld and System: A Critique of Functionalist Reason*, tr. Thomas McCarthy (Boston: Beacon Press, 1987).
15. MacIntyre, *After Virtue*, p. 24.

Index